Hope in Times of Horror

Memoirs of the Liberian Uncivil War

Quemiline Bull

ISBN 979-8-89043-106-6 (paperback)
ISBN 979-8-89043-107-3 (digital)

Christian Faith Publishing
832 Park Avenue
Meadville, PA 16335
www.christianfaithpublishing.com

Printed in the United States of America

This book is dedicated to my mother, Martha Dweda Bull, who was so suddenly separated from me and my family during the civil war in Liberia. Your legacy will always be with us.

Contents

Deuteronomy 4:9 ESV

"Only take care, and keep your soul dili-
gently, lest you forget the things that your eyes
have seen, and lest they depart from your heart
all the days of your life. Make them known to
your children and your children's children."

Preface

Growing up in Liberia, I experienced what I can only describe as a tropical paradise. I grew up in an environment where I was innocent and protected by my parents from every form of negative situation that I could have experienced. Life was a joy. The beautiful weather, the beautiful beaches, and having fun with friends in my neighborhood were only a part of the amazing life that I was living in Liberia. However, within a moment, my life changed for the worse. The negative experiences that I encountered impacted my life forever. I lost my mother. I eventually lost my uncle. I personally witnessed many forms of violence. All of this occurred because of a series of events that transferred from the foundation of Liberia. The painful history of the relationship between the free slaves (Congo/Americo-Liberians) and the indigenous Liberians and infighting between various indigenous tribes created a lasting challenge that unfortunately affected Liberia for years to come. The past eventually caught up with the present, and it led to the Liberian uncivil war. This book takes a look at my life growing up in Liberia and my experiences during the civil war. It also discusses my experience about getting to know and trust in God, the power of forgiveness, and the faithfulness of God in my life. This book is from the perspective of a preteen boy who suddenly found himself in an unusual environment. It tells of the impact that the civil war had in his life.

Acknowledgment

I would like to express my sincere thanks to my father, John
Emerson Bull Sr., for leading me through those difficult moments
that I experienced during the civil war and agreeing to sacrifice his
successful career to afford my brothers and me the opportunities that
we have come to enjoy today in the United States. I would also like
to express thanks and appreciation to my church, Redeem Christian
Church of God: Living Spring York Parish, and senior pastor Dr. Sola
Osundeko for inviting me to a conference from which the idea of this
book was birthed. I would also like to thank all of those who encouraged me to write this book, including my wife and my daughters. I
certainly gained strength from all the encouragement that I received
during the process of writing this book. Most importantly, I thank
God for giving me the strength and the ability to write this book, as

I revisited those painful memories that I experienced many years ago. While the memories of the war are painful, I believe that it was necessary to revisit those memories so that I could present an accurate narrative of my experiences and the impact of the war on my life.

Introduction

I was born in the Republic of Liberia, a small country located on the west coast of Africa. Like most individuals, I am proud of where I have come from. I enjoyed many wonderful moments during my childhood in Liberia. However, life can sometimes throw a curveball. Before going any further, I believe that it is important to take a look at the early history of Liberia.

Various indigenous tribal groups as far back as the twelfth century occupied the nation of Liberia (Dunn-Marcos et al 2005, 5). Between 1461 and the seventeenth century, several Europeans, such as the Dutch, British, and Portuguese, travelled to Liberia to trade (Dunn-Marcos et al 2005, 6). Meanwhile in the United States of America, the American government was abolishing slavery, and some thought it would be wise to repatriate free people of African descent back to the continent of Africa. In 1816, the American Colonization Society (ACS) was founded to carry out the mission of repatriating free Blacks back to the continent of Africa to avoid and escape racial discrimination in America (Dunn-Marcos et al 2005, 8). By 1822, the American Colonization Society started to send free Blacks to Africa. The land known today as Liberia was the location chosen for the free black slaves to be sent to (Dunn-Marcos et al 2005, 8).

Initially, the indigenous people were opposed to the migration of free Blacks from the United States to Liberia. I recall learning about the indigenous people of Liberia and the free Blacks fighting during their early introduction to one another. The free Blacks that were repatriated to Liberia from the United States were also referred to as Americo-Liberians. I recall learning about battles between the Americo-Liberians and the indigenous Liberians in elementary school. One story in particular was about how Matilda Newport, an Americo-Liberian, saved her fellow Americo-Liberians from the indigenous Liberians by shooting canons at the indigenous people and stopped them from overrunning the Americo-Liberian's settlement (Huffman 2004, 47). A holiday was also named after Matilda Newport as a result of her actions against the indigenous Liberians. History shows that the relationship between the Americo-Liberians and the indigenous Liberians was likely strained because the Americo-Liberians were forced upon the indigenous Liberians by the United States. According to early Liberian history, Chief Peter was persuaded to sell Cape Montserado to expand Americo-Liberians colony by pointing a pistol to his head (Bayard 1856, 46). It appeared that the contention in the very early relationship between the Americo-Liberians and the indigenous Liberians would have a negative impact on the nation of Liberia many years later. Finally, in 1847, Liberia became an independent nation.

The Americo-Liberians, also referred to as the Congo people, did not get along with the indigenous tribal people of Liberia at the early establishment of Liberian nation. The Americo-Liberians, backed by the US government, were more educated and saw themselves better than the indigenous people who did not have Western education, wear Western clothing, and spoke English. The Americo-Liberians created an elite group that excluded the indigenous Liberians. The Americo-Liberians created a single political party called the True Whig Party that only accepted Americo-Liberians into the party. That meant only Americo-Liberians were allowed to vote or hold political offices. Later on, as the nation progressed, small number of indigenous people was allowed into the upper class. This usually occurred if an indigenous Liberian obtained higher Western education, usually in the United States or married into an Americo-Liberian family. The latter was much difficult to accomplish and has been source of a lot of pain in the lives of quite a few women of indigenous Liberian background. During the early stages of Liberia, Americo-Liberians discriminated against indigenous Liberians based on class, and they strongly resisted becoming one with the indigenous Liberians.

Unfortunately, the party was known to be highly corrupt. They kept the wealth of the nation for the few elite Americo-Liberians (Dunn-Marcos et al 2005, 5). Slavery or forced labor occurred during the reign of the Americo-Liberians (Dunn-Marcos et al 2005, 14). The corruption was so widespread within Liberia that it was recognized internationally for its corruption by the *Guinness Book of Records*. According to the *Guinness Book of Records*, Liberia's seventeenth president Charles D. B. King was recognized for winning the most fraudulent presidential election in history. According to the official election result, President King received 234,000 votes. However, the nation of Liberia had only 15, 000 registered voters (Harris 2020, 4).

The historical oppression by the Americo-Liberians of the indigenous people of Liberia eventually lead to the coup d'état that was carried out by Master Sergeant Samuel Kanyon Doe. Master Sergeant Doe lead some soldiers, mostly members of the indigenous tribes of Liberia, to attack the Liberian executive mansion on April 12, 1980. This violent coup resulted in the murder of President William R. Tolbert Jr. Many True Whig Party members, who were government officials and also part of the Americo-Liberian community, were publicly humiliated and murdered by firing squad. Many members of the Americo-Liberian community had to flee Liberia for their safety.

Master Sergeant Doe eventually became the twenty-first president of Liberia. President Doe presidency ended the ruling of the elite Americo-Liberians. As the first president of Liberia to be from an indigenous tribe, there was high hope that President Doe would put an end to corruption and take care of the needs of the indigenous people that had been forsaken for many years. However, President Doe continued to do what the Americo-Liberians had done years before. President Doe created an elite society comprising of members from his tribe, the Krahn ethnic group. It was widely known that many of President Doe's government officials and a large majority of the members of the Armed Forces of Liberia were from the Krahn ethnic group. The actions of President Doe caused him to become very unpopular among the people of Liberia. The people of Liberia wanted a new leader. In 1985, President Doe granted the people of

Liberia the opportunity to choose a new leader. The election was held, and President Doe won the election. However, it was highly believed that the election was anything but fair.

The people of Liberia continue to revolt. University of Liberia students demonstrated in opposition to the election results. Finally, on November 12, 1985, one of President Doe's former associates, Gen. Thomas Quiwonkpa, attempted a coup d'état to remove President Doe from office. The coup d'état was originally believed to be successful. However, it later became clear that the coup d'état coup was a failure, and General Quiwonkpa was caught and murdered. In retaliation to the attack against him by General Quiwonkpa, President Doe punished the tribesmen of General Quiwonkpa in Nimba County. It was said that President Doe instructed his soldiers to travel to Nimba County and commit genocide against the Gio and Mano ethnic group. Unfortunately, this very act would be repeated many years later in the bloody Liberian civil war.

Early Childhood Memories

I was born in Monrovia, the capital city of Liberia, at the St. Joseph Catholic Hospital. By the grace of God, I was born to two wonderful parents, John Emerson Bull Sr. and Martha Dweda Bull. I resided in a small home, located on the campus of the A. M. Dogliotti College of Medicine. My family was able to reside at that location because my father was the dean of administration at the medical college. Honestly, it was one of the best places to live. It was located within a mile from the shores of the Atlantic Ocean. My home was also located a few yards away from the St. Joseph Catholic Hospital, where my brothers and I were born. My neighborhood also hosted the embassies of many nations from around the world. Some of the countries that had embassies in my neighborhood included China, Japan, Egypt, Nigeria, and Germany. While there were many embassies in my neighborhood, my brothers and I did not get to hang out there a lot because our parents usually did not allow us out of their sight. My neighborhood also included a large expatriate community. I had neighbors from the United States, Korea, Philippines, Netherlands, Ireland, Spain, Germany, and Lebanon to name a few. My environment created the opportunity for me to meet lots of people from all around the world, especially other children who I got to know and play with. My experiences in interacting with so many different people from such widely diverse cultures led me to become interested in traveling and learning about different cultures from around the world. I enjoyed playing soccer with my friends in the neighborhood, meeting new friends from around the world and also the local children. The only negative was that it was often upsetting to lose friends whose parents were embassy employees and had to leave because of reassignment. It helped that I spoke English, which made it easier to communicate with so many different people from around the world. Actually, most Liberians speak English, which is very convenient since there are approximately sixteen different dialects that are spoken in Liberia.

While most of the nation of Liberia is rural, Monrovia contained the only major urban community during my childhood. I remember that it was always exciting to go to the city with my parents to visit relatives or go shopping. However, I lived in the outskirts of the city, so my community was less active than the city. I still enjoyed living in the suburbs and climbing trees to pick almond, mango, and coconut. Unfortunately, I would sometimes encounter wildlife, which was something that I would rather not experience in a close encounter. I remember an incident when I was climbing a coconut tree in front of my house and I came face-to-face with a green snake. I was shocked, and I immediately jumped out of the tree. Luckily for me, it was not one of the usual tall coconut trees in the yard. I'm not a big fan of snakes, and I do my best to avoid them. However, I would have a few more encounters with them. It seemed like the fear of snakes did not keep us away from trees. My brothers and I were always picking nuts and fruits from trees in our neighborhood. Those trees acted as our private vending machines that provided us with all the snacks that we needed. There were several palm trees beside my home. There were also plenty of plantain trees and a few pawpaw (papaya) trees behind my house. How could I forget the infamous guava tree. This tree was bittersweet. While the guava from the tree was very tasty, the tree branch was a very good tool for disciplining little children. Trust me, I know this very well because I had a lot of experience with the guava tree branch. The trees also beautified out community. I remember that the road leading to the beach had coconut trees on both sides of the road. During the Christmas season, all of the trees were painted with white paint around the bottom. It created such a wonderful view and it truly felt like the most wonderful time of the year. During the Christmas season, our parents usually got my brothers and I a gift. The gift was usually something that we really needed.

My parents were both government employees. As I stated earlier, my father worked at the medical college. My mother worked for the Liberian National Police (LNP). So both of my parents worked for government agencies. Under the administration of President Doe, government employees were not paid regularly. For this reason, my family, like many families in Liberia who were not connected to those in power, struggled to make ends meet. I recall getting pulled out of class a few times because of unpaid tuition. Liberia does not have a public school system. You either have the funds to pay tuition for your child or your child does not receive an education. This was, and still is, one of the many challenges that I believe is preventing the growth of the nation. In spite of the financial challenges that my parents experienced, they always made sure that my siblings and me had what we needed. In fact, many of my neighborhood friends would state that my parents had a lot of money. After all, my brothers and I always wore clean clothes and attended very good schools, and we did not have to be involved in child labor like some of the kids in my neighborhood. I can understand why they would come to that conclusion, given the examples that I just highlighted. However, that was far from the truth. Unfortunately, child labor continues to be an act that is still practiced today in Liberia. I am grateful to have been blessed to have had such wonderful parents who were committed to providing the best care that my brothers and I could have received. I am not sure how they did it, given the various challenges that they faced. I believed that they definitely had no choice but to depend on God for provision.

My mother was a very devoted Christian, and she was very active in church. She sang in the choir at St. Peter Lutheran Church, which my family attended. She would also prepare meals, especially pastries, as her contribution to events held at the church. I recall my mother baking for church events and me becoming upset at her for giving away all our tasty cakes. As a child, I did not understand the actions of my mother. I did not know that she was giving her time, money, energy, and talent for God's work to be done. However, I now appreciate and currently contribute to the church as she had done. It is certainly one of those things that I have learned from her that has been helpful in my current life. I hope someday to pass on this practice of contributing to the church to my children. My mother did not only contribute to the church, but she also encouraged my siblings and me to attend church. While she did not insist that we attend service along with her, she did insist that we attend church on Sundays. Fortunately, there was no shortage of churches in my neighborhood. I was fond of two of the churches in my community. One of those churches was the Philadelphia Church. I liked this church because the Sunday-school teachers told Bible stories in a way that was very exciting. The only challenge was that on our way to Philadelphia church, my brothers and I had to walk past several expatriates' homes. Many of those homes had dogs that would bark at us as we walk past their homes. Fortunately for us, many of their homes had fences. I recall vividly how I was tormented by those German shepherds. German shepherds seemed to be the popular dogs in my neighborhood. A US senior military officer who lived at the last expatriate house owned a bulldog. I was unfamiliar with this breed of dog; therefore, I was very afraid of it. Although we were afraid of the dogs, we still continued to attend church at Philadelphia because it allowed us to get home early.

We also attended the Assembly of God church, which was established by United States evangelist Jimmy Swaggart. The Assembly of God church was much closer than Philadelphia church. It was so close to my home that I could see the large yellow-and-white tent where the revival crusade was held from my back porch. I was introduced to the Assembly of God church because my mother took my sibling and me there to attend the crusade. My mother also took us to the revival because she was desperately looking for healing for my older brother who was hearing and speech impaired. I remember following my mother to many revivals as she looked for divine healing for my older brother. Unfortunately, my mother did not get to see my brother gain his speech and hearing.

My brothers and I chose to attend church close to home because we were able to get home earlier after church. There were lot of benefits for getting home early on a Sunday in Liberia when I was growing up. The weekends in Liberia was usually a time of relaxation, a time for family and close friends to spend more time together. Usually,

4

during Sundays, the best meals were cooked. Families also invited or visited special guests to spend time watching a good movie together. If you weren't doing any of these things, you were probably spending time playing with your neighborhood friends or spending time with your family on the beaches.

My childhood was great, and my family and I were very content with our lives in spite of the financial challenges we faced. As a child, there was so much to enjoy, such as family and the natural environment. It was always fun when my paternal grandmother, who we called Old Ma, came to visit. She was such a strong woman, and she loved us boys very much. She always brought treats from her farm in the interior whenever she came to visit. Although she was a grandmother, she was strong and independent. I recall my mother asking my grandmother to come and live with us in the city several times. However, my grandmother always declined the offer from my mother. I must admit that my grandmother's action was very unusual as it was common for individuals her age to live with their adult children, especially if their children were capable of taking care of them. I also remember my maternal uncles who would come to visit us from the interior parts of Liberia. As was customary, my relatives usually brought gifts. My uncles would often bring with them goats or chickens, which we often killed and prepared in our backyard. Often, delicious meals were prepared when close friends and relatives came to visit. I have many fond memories of relatives and friends coming to visit as it was a time for my brothers and me to play with friends and cousins. We often played a game of cops and robbers or the war game. Basically, the war game was a game of two groups hunting each other. Whoever said "pow pow" first killed their opponent. This was the most popular game played by children in Monrovia. I'm quite sure that the war game was popular in all of Liberia. The war game was influenced by American action films such as *Rambo*, which starred Sylvester Stallone; *First Blood*, which starred Chuck Norris; and *Commando*, which starred Arnold Schwarzenegger. The games were mostly played among young boys; but girls sometimes joined in the fun. These games made up for great memories that sometimes cause me to burst into sudden smile.

5

(Pre-Civil War Photos of Family and Friends)

(Pre-Civil War Photos of Family and Friends)

(Pre-Civil War Photos of Family and Friends)

(Pre-Civil War Photos of Family and Friends)

(Pre-Civil War Photos of Family and Friends)

(Pre-Civil War Photos of Family and Friends)

1989: Normal Life Ends

The year of 1988 ended. As usual, the end of the year, which is the Christmas season, is a very festive time in Liberia. My parents give us Christmas presents, which usually consisted of items that we needed for school. Sometimes we got clothes since we were always growing. I remember that year, for our Christmas presents, my mother bought my brothers and me some cool high-top sneakers. My younger brother and I got a similar pair of sneakers. My older brother got a pair sneakers that was so cool that he became like a star among our peers. They were so cool looking that we all wanted a pair. I don't even remember what they were called, but I can still remember what they looked like until now.

My siblings and I were very excited to return to school after the Christmas break. We were looking forward to displaying our new sneakers, or Christmas shoes as they were referred to in Liberia. My siblings and I were not alone. Actually, many of my schoolmates would return to school eager to display the various Christmas gifts that they had received from their parents and loved ones. While there were some kids whose parents had the means to provide whatever they wanted such as bikes and Nintendo video game, my brothers and I were not in the position to get what we wanted. However, we were grateful to be able to get what our parents provided for us. Fortunately for us, we were not among those children who did not have parents that could provide their basic needs such as good education, food, clothing, and healthcare. In Liberia, we had no system in place to provide us with those basic needs. If your parents could not afford them, you simply did not get them.

During the school year, I had a major experience that greatly impacted my life. I would describe the impact as one that was positive, although it did not appear to be so in the moment. During the early stages of my childhood, I experienced difficulty in learning. I was not very good in my schoolwork; therefore, my grades were not good. My father was often disappointed with my poor grades. I understood his frustration because he had high expectations for me. I also understood that my father could not have understood my challenge because he was very good in school. In spite of my struggles in school, I managed to pass to the next class at the end of the school year. My luck came to an unfortunate end in the fifth grade when I didn't make it to the next grade at the end of the school year. This time, I was unable to score just enough to make it to the next class. I was devastated; I literally became instantly ill. I'm not sure if the illness was due to my disappointment or fear of punishment from my parents. My parents did not punish me though. The simple expression of disappointment from my parents, relatives, and family friends had more of an impact on me than any spanking or pumping tire (squat) that I could have gotten. As a result of my failure, I became motivated to overcome the academic struggle that I was experiencing. I recall that in that year, the summer break seemed like it took forever. I was eager to return to school and face the academic challenge in my life, and I was determined to overcome. Eventually, school reopened, and I returned to school optimistic about the new school year. When I returned to school, I came across a whole new set of challenges. I encountered my former classmates who decided to make me the object of ridicule because I had to repeat the fifth grade. I was not surprised, because immature youth would often indulge in such behavior. This was the culture of students in Liberia at the time. In spite of all that I had to endure, I continued to focus on proving myself to all of those who were disappointed in me and had ridiculed me. I worked hard and attended after-school study class to help me improve in my schoolwork.

I finally made it through the first marking period, and I did just what I had planned to do. I overcame my academic challenge, and I scored pretty high marks in all subjects except Bible. I believed that

I overlooked Bible because I thought that I would pass the subject since I was very familiar with Bible. After all, I was always in church, and Bible was not a challenging class anyway. I put a lot of focus on those subjects that presented challenges to me such as math and science. Unfortunately, I overlooked Bible. Regardless, I was proud of myself.

As I stated earlier, this experience was very impactful in my life. I learned three very important lessons from this experience. The first lesson that I learned was to get back up after falling. This is a lesson that I've come to appreciate as life is full of ups and downs. My second lesson was to always be hopeful because situations could change for the better. Developing the ability to face and overcome challenges that I've encountered in life is something that had helped me greatly in my life. The third lesson that I've come to learn is to do things my way. I quickly realized that one of the reasons that I was having trouble in school was because the method used to teach me was not compatible to my way of learning. I made the decision to study and learn in ways that were suitable for me. Learning to do things in ways that work best for me individually proved to be successful. It showed in my grades when I received my report card. Once I experienced success after changing my technique, I began to believe that success was achievable for me.

The year of 1989 was full of surprises. I learned that my mother, who was in her final year at the University of Liberia, was pregnant. I remembered that she was very excited about her pregnancy. She believed that she was finally going to have a daughter. All along she had been hoping for a daughter; but instead, she had birthed three stubborn sons who believed that they were WWF (World Wrestling Federation) superstars. I was told by some of my aunts that my mother strongly believed that her second pregnancy would have produced a daughter but instead, she got me. I remembered that everyone in my home was really excited for mother. We all knew how much she wanted a daughter, and we were happy that she was finally going to get her wishes come true. I was not sure how she had come to the determination that she was having a girl. After all, ultrasound technology was not available in Liberia at the time. Nevertheless, we were all very happy for my mother, and I guess it would have been fun to have a little sister. Looking back, I believed that my mother's faith in God was the basis of her claim.

The year of 1989 seemed very promising. After all, I had finally overcome my academic challenge by improving my grades, and I was also expecting a baby sister. That year I started to get into a little bit of martial arts and weightlifting with my uncle Nana. I also began learning the game of basketball. My favorite ice cream shop, Sophie's Ice Cream, had concluded renovation with many upgrades to enjoy. At the moment, I was living life with so much enthusiasm and looking forward to enjoying all the exciting and positive changes in my life. It appeared that my life was moving in the right direction. In spite of the corruption within the Liberian government and all of the challenges that the people of Liberia were facing during that time, there were some signs of improvement in Liberia.

Besides the upgrade to Sophie's Ice Cream, our nation's soccer team was beginning to be a bright star in Africa. The Liberia Lone Star's success brought a sense of pride to all Liberians. There were also new buildings that were been erected by the government. We also experienced improvement in our own family. My parents purchased a piece of land that year so that we could build our home. I went along with my parents to the Duport Road community to take a look at the land. I remembered looking at the blueprint for the house and feeling so excited that we would be moving into a new home.

In all, the year 1989 seemed to be going very well. Life appeared to be so much fun. In fact, my last activity of 1989 was my attendance of a hip-hop concert at Sophie's Ice Cream Shop. Hip-hop was starting to become popular in Liberia. Many of the older kids followed and idolized hip-hop artist like Fat Boys, Heavy D, Big Daddy Kane, LL Cool J, Run DMC, Salt and Pepper, etc. I attended the concert with my uncle Nana, who was also performing that day. My uncle Nana, whose last name is Scott, went by the stage name Scott the Rock. I'm sure that his stage name was influenced by the late DJ Scott La Rock, the American hip-hop artist. The name suited Uncle Nana very well since his last name was Scott and he was a bodybuilder. My uncle Nana was very influential in my life. I idolized him as a young boy, and I did all that I could do to be like him. Now, as an adult, I still see his influence in my life when I lift weights and play basketball.

The year 1989 ended very well. I was very excited about leaving the eighties and stepping into the nineties. I saw it as an opportunity to step into a new beginning, a new beginning that would be full of successes. However, life sometimes throws us a curveball.

The Fall

After returning home from the hip-hop concert with my uncle Nana, I saw my dad and some of the men in the neighborhood gathered around the radio. While this was not unusual, it was pretty uncommon to see adults gathered around the radio around the Christmas season. I often saw adults gathered around the radio to listen to soccer matches or listening to important political events such as election results or politician speeches. While there was television service available in Liberia at the time, it provided limited service. There was only one state-ran television station, which was called ELBC. ELBC operated between 6:00 p.m. to 12:00 a.m. Therefore, the radio provided better source of communication since it allowed its users access to multiple channels such as BBC (British Broadcasting Corporation) News. It was uncommon to see people huddle around the radio during that era because Christmas was a very festive time in Liberia. During the Christmas season, people were usually eating and the adults were enjoying Club beer, playing Ludo (Parcheesi), or listening to Christmas music. Liberians would usually not be listening to politics around the Christmas season. It was a time for celebration, eating, socializing, and shopping. However, I noticed that my father and the men, who were on the back porch of my home, seemed very focused on the news. It appeared that there was something serious going on. I don't remember all the details. However, I do remember my father and his friends talking about a military attack. I recalled them saying that a Liberian military group came from Ivory Coast and entered Liberia through Nimba County. For me, as an eleven-year-old boy, my perception of war was very far from reality. I

17

believed war to be very similar to the action films that I was used to watching. I actually thought that we the people were going to be in no danger. I simply thought that the soldiers were going to meet on the major road and fight among themselves.

My parents did not speak to us much about what was going on. I am sure that they wanted to preserve our childhood and keep us from worrying. After all, Christmas was less than twenty-four hours away. Everything was going on normally in my community; therefore, there was no cause for concern. We wanted to celebrate the Christmas holiday and enjoy our Christmas break from school. For us kids, everything appeared to be going on as it normally did. I could not help but notice that my parents and their friends were unusually interested in what was being said on the 5:00 p.m. BBC news. My mother did an excellent job of keeping my brothers and I distracted from the concerns of a civil war. My mother was able to distract my brothers and I by having us write letters to my aunt in England. According to my mother, she wanted us to include in the letter our Christmas wishes for the next Christmas season. This was a very successful strategy because it kept us occupied for a very long period of time. We would make long list of things that we wanted such as jeans, T-shirt, British Knights sneakers, and a variety of toys. I am quite sure that none of those letters ever got mailed to my aunt in England. My mother's plan kept us occupied and gave the adults the privacy that they needed to discuss their concerns about what the war would mean for everyone.

So the year ended, and we moved into a new decade. After all, I had lived most of my life in the eighties, and I was excited to be going into nineties. The Christmas break ended, and I returned to school. I was really excited to be back in school, not only to see my friends but also to prove to myself that I could be a good student. School was no longer burdensome for me because I had overcome my academic challenges. After returning to school for the first few months, every-thing still seemed normal. However, I started to learn more about the war by listening to the news and from adult conversations. The news was everywhere, and my parents could no longer shield me from news of the civil war. During those days, it seemed like politics and war were all everyone talked about. It didn't take long before I started to notice a change in my neighborhood. I started to see more new people in my neighborhood. I later learned that these were people fleeing the fighting and moving away to safety.

I recalled that we had a scare one day at school. I remember that we were in class, and the teachers were panicking, trying to gather us all together. The teachers were attempting to take us to safety because there was rumor that members of the rebel forces had entered the city. Luckily for us, the news was false, and my schoolmate and I were not in immediate danger. While that situation was only a scare, the incident brought to reality the challenges that the civil war was having on the everyday lives of those residing in Liberia, especially those of us in the capital city of Monrovia. In spite of the challenges, we continued to attend school. The question began to be asked as to when school would be closed. It was apparent that life in the city was tense and getting dangerous. Parents were concerned about their children's safety, and they did not want their children to be at risk of experiencing harm. Not long after the scare at my school, schools started to shut down in Monrovia. I am sure that this brought relief to my parents as the uncertainty of the civil war had destabilized the safety of the public. Soldiers began to appear all around us. They often looked tense and very aggressive. Members of the public were afraid of these soldiers because they were known to be very brutal. The soldiers often carried guns, and they did whatever they wanted. It was pretty standard in Liberia for those in position of authority to misuse their authority. Coincidentally, this is what led to the issue of corruption in Liberia. Corruption was the major catalyst for the civil war that was on going.

Fighting in Monrovia

School closed prematurely around the end of the first quarter of the year. Usually, when school would close, it would be a time of fun and excitement for me. While I did have some fun in the beginning of school closing because I still had the opportunity to play with friends in my neighborhood and spent more time with my family, it did not last very long. I started to miss my friends at school. I also lost contact with close friends and relatives. Due to civil war, I was unable to take regular family vacations such as going to Buchanan in Grand Bassa County to visit relatives. My parents also did not want to risk us going to town in central Monrovia either and getting stuck. So we stayed close to home.

During this time, my family tried to live life as normally as possible. This became difficult to do as the effects of the war started to rapidly approach my home city of Monrovia. We started to directly experience the effect of the civil war when we started to lose essential services provided by the government. We lost electricity as members of the rebel group called NPFL (National Patriotic Front of Liberia) advanced toward the capital city of Monrovia. As the government was preoccupied with protecting the presidency of Samuel Doe, the nation was shutting down every major operation that was producing income for Liberia. Firestone, which operated in Liberia and was a major producer of rubber, could not operate due to the civil conflict. Other major corporations operating in Liberia such as LAMCO, an iron ore mining company, and other logging companies had to shut down. Most of the managers of those companies, who were foreigners, fled Liberia for their own safety. Everyone was trying to get out of Liberia at the time. After all, the news that we were receiving from BBC news reporters and other sources of international news were very discouraging. There was news of tribal killings by members of the NPFL. These NPFL members, who were mostly from the Gio and Mano tribes from Nimba County, were said to be seeking and killing members of President Doe's tribesmen who were from the Krahn tribe. NPFL members were also seeking members of the Mandingo tribe. There was also news of mass casualty among members of the Liberian population due to aggressive fighting between the government forces and the NPFL forces.

One of the stories that stuck with me until now is a story that I heard my mother talking about regarding a report that she heard on the news. According to my mother, she heard of a story where an infant's mother had been killed on the battlefield between the government forces and NPFL forces. The NPFL forces had just taken over the town where infant and their mother must have lived. According to my mother, the reporter stated that the infant was observed crawling on the mother and attempting to get to the mother's breast as everyone was fleeing from the battlefield. I started to think as to why someone did not go back and get the infant. It is also possible that in that chaotic situation, those fleeing the town could not have realized that the child was there. Maybe the situation did not allow for someone to go back and risk losing their own life. Although I never got to find out the outcome of that child, I started to become very concerned about the disaster that awaited us.

The civil war also led to a medical emergency, as large groups of people started to move into Monrovia, which created overcrowding. As more people moved into the city, there became a shortage of supplies, such as food, firewood, charcoal, and medication. We also lost access to clean drinking water as news of the Doe regime poisoning the water system of Liberia came to light. Not long after the news of the Doe regime poisoning the water, our water supply was shut off. It was rumored that President Doe and his supporters shut the water supply to punish the Liberian people, who were believed to be in support of the president's removal from office. The lack of safe drinking water led to a cholera and dysentery outbreak, which killed many Liberians. Cholera is an infection that results in a diarrhea-like reaction that causes a person to lose weight and die in a short period of time. I recall that we had to boil our water before drinking. Due to lack of running water in our home, my brothers and I had to help out and fetch water for our home from the wells. Looking back, I can now see that I developed my work ethics during these difficult times. It was developed under a desperate need for survival. While finding water was very challenging, transporting it was even more challenging. At first, my uncle, my older brother, and I were able to get water from a well located at the Getty Lou Flower Park Resort located near the St. Joseph Catholic Hospital. I used to walk approximately half a mile to fetch water, and I would have to carry the water in a five-gallon container. It was quite a challenge, but I had to do what I had to do. I understood that it was necessary for me to help my family. After all, we needed water to carry out our everyday affairs. It was then that I became aware of how significant water was to my daily life. I also appreciated much more the opportunity that I once had of having water supply in my home. As time went by, life became extremely dangerous.

It became very dangerous for us to venture away from our home. More people were randomly getting killed by members of the Armed Forces of Liberia (AFL). It even became risky for us to go out and get water for our family. Although it was risky to go out in the evening to fetch water like we used to do, we had no other alternative. We could not function as a family without the basic need of water. Therefore, we had to continue to take the risk to leave home and fetch water. Fortunately, my uncle Nana was able to find a path through the bushes to get to the well. It was a shorter route, but it was difficult, especially for me as an eleven-year-old kid at the time. Carrying a five-gallon container that weighed approximately forty pounds for an approximately eighty-pound boy was very tasking. It was even more tasking because the new route required me to walk up a hill that was very steep. I had to climb this steep hill with my brother and uncle to get to the asphalt road that led to my home. The trip was made even more difficult because I wore rubber flip-flops when I carried out my chores. Although I had other shoes, they were reserved for other activities such as church and schools. That allowed our shoes to last a little longer. Often, my flip-flop would get wet from carrying the water, and it made it so much more difficult for me to walk in them. My feet would consistently slide out of the flip-flop, especially when I attempted to climb the steep hill. However, I had to hurry as I did not want to get caught out in the bushes by soldiers. I did not want to find out what would have happened to me or my brother and uncle.

In spite of the difficulties that I had to endure to get water, I was still grateful that I even had access to water. Many of the people in Monrovia at the time could not find clean drinking water. This was a major cause of the epidemic that resulted in the death of many people. Having lived across the street from the St. Joseph Catholic Hospital, I had the unfortunate experience of seeing the sorrow many experienced after losing their loved ones. Often, I would witness families and friends carrying their loved ones to the hospital in a wheelbarrow or vehicle to seek medical treatment. A few minutes later, I would see the same individuals wailing as they are leaving the hospital, sometimes with their loved ones and sometimes without them. I'm sure that the supplies at the hospital had to be limited, I don't believe that the hospital was prepared to deal with the heavy increase in the number of patients that they were receiving. What was even more challenging was that they were unable to receive new supplies. I'm sure that every medical facility in Liberia was experiencing the same.

The people of Liberia later received a saving grace after a nongovernmental foreign organization called Medicine San Frontier (MSF) came to Liberia to assist in providing much needed medical services to suffering people in Liberia. The group comprised of European doctors that provided medical treatment at no cost to the people of Liberia. They also provided food supplies as well. At the time, my father, being one of the leaders of the community, assisted the MSF staff settle in our community. It made sense to establish MSF in our community since the hospital and medical school were already there. That meant more help would become available in terms of manpower and equipment. Although they settled in my community, they travelled all over the city of Monrovia providing medical services to various communities and medical facilities. They even provided medical assistance to members of the Armed Forces of Liberia that were brought to the hospital because of injuries received on the battlefield.

I recalled my father being very busy during those times. He played a major role in organizing the workers to assist with unloading medical supplies and food into the medical college campus. He also collaborated with St. Joseph Catholic Hospital staff to store the supplies provided by MSF. My father was very committed to improving the well-being of the people in the community. My father was doing all this work during a time when he was not receiving a paycheck from the government. Obviously, the government was in disarray dealing with a civil war. Yet my father continued to work to make life better for those within our community, sometime even at the point of risking his life. In spite of the challenges that he faced to provide and protect his family, he continued to assist MSF in working to ensure that the needs of the people in the community were met. The assistance provided by many of the nongovernmental organizations such as MSF and the United Nations greatly reduced the death rate in Liberia.

The situation in Liberia continued to worsen rapidly as the months went by. We had lost electricity. Now we were out of two major essential services that would negatively impact our livelihoods for the unforeseeable future. Not only were we without water, now we did not have electricity. The absence of electricity created a whole new set of challenges for me. For the first time, I came to experience what total darkness at night looked like. Whenever I went out to the back of the house at night, it was completely dark, with no electricity at all. Now the hospital did have electricity, but we had no access to it. For the rest of us locals, we simply had to deal with the darkness. We had to depend on candles and kerosene lantern to be able to see at night. My uncle Nana was a great help to our family. He would get charcoal for my mother to cook. Charcoal quickly became short because most people were using charcoal to cook. We had to transition to using wood to cook—that is, if you could find it. We also had no way of preserving food since we had no electricity. Therefore, we had to eat most of what we had daily. My mother did what she could to preserve raw meat and fish using spices, but that usually only lasted a day or two. With each moment, things seemed to continue to get worse. Losing significant resources such as water and electricity came to be the least of our worries as the war continued.

Death Squad

As the civil war progressed, we began to hear stories of violence being committed by members of the Armed Forces of Liberia. This was no surprise to many of those living in Liberia as the Liberian national forces already had a history of committing violence against its citizens. One of such acts was the killing of former president Tolbert. The violence of President Doe's soldiers was also made visible when members of President Tolbert's cabinet were murdered in public view by firing squad during the coup d'état. So many Liberians expected some violence from the government forces soldiers. Many Liberians did not anticipate the extreme violence that would come to be. As a child, I feared those soldiers because they carried long rifles and long cutlasses. The facial expressions of the government forces soldiers were very intimidating, and many were certainly looking to intimidate the people of Liberia. During one incident, I was on my way home from my cousin's house in Cabral Estate with my uncle Nana and my brothers when we came across a government forces soldier. We were travelling on foot like many Liberians did during that time. There was a sense of tension in the air. It was not the exciting and peaceful environment that I had grown up in. While walking, my uncle Nana told us to be careful. It appeared that my uncle did not want to get the soldier's attention. He was trying to avoid the soldier by all means necessary. Unfortunately, we had to cross path with the soldier. When we came close to the soldier, I understood why my uncle was attempting to evade the soldier. The soldier was not only carrying an assault rifle on his shoulder, but he was also carrying a machete in his hand. The look on the soldier's face gave me the feeling that he was going to cause us harm or death. I was praying in my heart that the soldier did not stop us or call us over to him. Fortunately, the soldier did not stop us or harm us. This was yet another reminder of the constant state of fear that we were living in at the time—fear that would accompany the civil conflict that I now found myself in. As the war continued and Charles Taylor's rebel forces advanced on the capital of Liberia, President Doe issued a curfew. I had never heard of a curfew, nor did I know what the word meant. However, I quickly became familiar with the word as curfew would become a part of life for a while. I remembered that in the evenings, the streets were cleared of all citizens. Only members of President Doe's government forces could be seen patrolling the streets of Monrovia. My parents ensured that we were all indoors before the curfew started. We did not want to discover through experience what the government forces soldiers would do to us if we violated their curfew policy. However, I had the unfortunate experience of observing how members of President Doe's government forces handled curfew violators. One evening, I was standing on the back porch at my house, looking at Tubman Boulevard and watching the cars drive by like I usually do. However, this time there were only soldiers driving by. As I was looking, I saw a gentleman walking, who I immediately identified as Chief, a homeless man who was mentally incapable of making sound decisions. He was well-known within the community. My father used to provide him with assistance all of the time. I immediately became afraid for his safety. I feared what would happen if members of the government forces came across him. It did not take long before a group of soldiers in a convoy came across him. As I watched from my back porch, the soldiers slowed down their vehicles. I am quite sure that they were questioning him about violating the curfew. Shortly after the initial encounter, I heard the sound of gun fire, and I saw Chief falling to the ground. For the first time in my life, I had witnessed the murder of a person. Sadly, there would be more of such experiences to come. I also later discovered that the soldiers who murdered Chief were known as the Death Squad. They were known to be President Doe's special unit who served at his direct command. The group was known to be led by General Tilly, a merciless soldier who was known to kill anyone that he pointed his silver pistol at. General Michael Tilly was known to have personally killed multiple Liberians. What I had just noticed exposed me to what war was really like. I feared the new reality that I had come to find myself in. From what I had just witnessed, anyone could be subject to senseless murder. A reality that was once of innocence, joy, and peace was now turning into a reality of danger, fear, and murders.

As the war continued, there continued to be more news of murders and violence by members of the Armed Forces of Liberia. The situation in Liberia was quickly going out of control. The increase in the murders within Monrovia was because of the genocide that was occurring at the hands of the government forces, which were mostly from the Krahn ethnic group. President Doe's soldiers (mostly Krahns) and members of the Mandingo tribe were seeking members of the Gio and Mano tribes from Nimba County. The differences between these two groups likely originated as a result of a failed coup attempt by Gen. Thomas Quiwonkpa, a native of Nimba County. General Quiwonkpa, who assisted President Doe gain power during the 1980 coup d'état, was killed; and President Doe was believed to have ordered his soldiers to torture the people of Nimba because of General Quiwonkpa's coup attempt.

Now the revolt against President Doe was led by Charles McArthur Taylor, another former member of President Doe's government. Charles Taylor was from Americo-Liberian ancestry. He sought the help of the people of Nimba County, who had been tormented by President Doe and his soldiers. Charles Taylor was pretty crafty in seeking the assistance of the people of Nimba County. He knew that their shared anger for President Doe would provide an abundance of motivation for his new soldiers to fervently battle the Armed Forces of Liberia. So the civil war was very connected to the past ills of Liberia. It was those past ills that influenced the actions of the government forces to commit genocide against the Congo, Gio, and Mano ethnic groups. Sadly, they were hunted like animals and killed, sometimes in large numbers, simply because of their ethnic backgrounds.

My family was hosting my father's friend and his family. They came to our home because it was near the hospital and it was considered a little safer than most communities in Monrovia. My father's friend's wife was from the Krahn ethnic group. My parents did all that they could to protect her. My parent feared that members of the community could try to out her identity when members of Charles Taylor's NPFL (National Patriotic Front of Liberia) captured Monrovia. So my father's friend wanted his wife to be in a different environment where no one would know her identity. Many others in Monrovia did similar things. Many people who were at risk of being killed because of their ethnicity sought refuge at the American embassy and other American establishments like Greystone compound. Others sought refuge at the St. Peter's Lutheran Church, which my family frequently attended for Sunday services.

In July of 1990, we received very devastating news on *BBC News*. We woke up one morning in July and started to hear rumors of another massacre that had occurred overnight at the St. Peter's Lutheran Church. There was news that during the night, some members of the Armed Forces of Liberia entered the compound of St. Peter's Lutheran Church and murdered members of the Gio and Mano ethnic group that were seeking refuge on the church property. We heard that the people, which included women and children, were hacked to death with machetes by President Doe's soldiers. Later, *BBC News* confirmed the unfortunate news. It was reported that approximately six hundred men, women, and children were either shot or hacked to death on that property by President Doe's government forces. It was also rumored that that this atrocity occurred with the Red Cross flag flying on the church property. However, as with many of the soldiers in Liberia, they had no regard for military laws or any other laws at all. They simply did what they wanted to do. We all simply existed by the grace of God because we were all exposed to mistreatment and danger from members of the government forces. There were countless stories of government soldiers harassing and mistreating members of the public. There was news of torturing and killing of people randomly for unjustifiable reasons. While acts of violence occurred all the time, the nighttime was the worst time. There was always the anticipation of soldiers knocking on our door in the middle of the night to harass us or murder us. Fortunately, I did not get to experience this during that time. My family did experience a visit from President Doe's elite soldiers known as the Death Squad on one hot and sunny afternoon. This would be a day that I would remember for the rest of my life.

That day started like any other day. I recalled my father and my mother discussing plans to kill and cook the few chickens that we were raising. There was shortage of food, and they realized that the chickens would soon all be stolen. These were desperate times, and people were certainly looking to take desperate measures. Also, my parents also believed that members of the government forces would soon help themselves to our chickens. So my uncle Nana and others gathered the few chickens that we had left and killed them to prepare a meal and also preserve some for a later time. I recalled that my mother cooked palm butter on that day. Palm butter was my favorite Liberian stew and the signature stew of my mother's tribal group. While my mother was cooking, a group of government forces soldiers came to our home and ordered us all to come out. When we all walked to the front yard, we noticed that all our neighbors were being gathered as well. There were several medical students and their families and other close friends gathered in front of the "Chicken Dorm." Some of the government soldiers went into our home and the homes of my neighbors. They usually did this to steal whatever they wanted from citizen's homes. We were all standing outside, scared and confused. The uncertainty was the worse. I did not know if the soldiers were going to kill us or remove us from our home. While we were standing outside under the heat of the afternoon sun, I noticed some of the soldiers walking out of our home eating the meal that my mother had just cooked. Some of the soldiers had also taken some of our belongings out of our home. During this time, we were guarded by soldiers who appeared very intimidating. After much moving around, a soldier, a brown-skinned man, walked to the front of us. I remembered that we were all standing in a sort of a formation. This particular soldier seemed to be the head of the group. I do not recall what he said, but I remembered that he asked several of my neighbors about what ethnic group that they belonged to. He even asked for identifications from us, and I presented my identification. Many of those born in Liberia had a national identification card that included our photo, name, and tribal ethnicity. After the soldiers checked our identifications, the leader of the group displayed a silver pistol and started speaking to the other soldiers in a dialect that I did not understand. I would guess that he was speaking Krahn since many of the members of the government forces were of the Krahn ethnic group. It appeared that he was giving the other soldiers some kind of instruction. During this time, I saw my father's friend's wife whisper to my mother that the soldiers were speaking her dialect. I saw my mother look at my father's friend's wife with urgency and whispered to her to speak to the soldiers in her dialect. Fortunately, my father's friend's wife quickly spoke to the soldiers in her native dialect. The leader of the group stopped speaking immediately and spoke something in his dialect. When the soldiers had realized that one of the citizens that they had just gathered was a member of their own tribal group, they changed their attitude toward us. The commanding officer put his pistol away and asked us if we needed anything. The other soldiers even stated that they wish that my father's friend's wife had spoken earlier, and some of the soldiers offered us kids a few coins. The soldiers also stopped eating our food, and they returned to us whatever was left of our meal. The soldiers left our home. This felt like such a close call. I later learned that those soldiers were members of the notorious Death Squad. I also later learned that leader of the group was General Tilly. It was commonly known that General Tilly rarely displayed his silver pistol without using it to take away a life. After learning how close I was to losing my life, I was grateful to God for saving me and my family. That afternoon God give me and my family another chance at life. In all likelihood, we were all probably going to be murdered on that hot sunny afternoon.

One thing that this incident did was to bring the danger of the war to our reality. Before, we heard about atrocities committed against fellow Liberians on the radio. Now we came to face harassment, hostility, and almost death by the soldiers that were supposed to protect us. Unfortunately, hatred, anger, and frustration lead to the creation of the circumstances that we were encountering. It was also obvious that lack of education and leadership highly contributed to the situation that we were facing in Liberia.

Captured

We did not know it, but the encounter with the Death Squad was a sign that the rebel forces were closing in on us. I remembered seeing more soldiers in my neighborhood with more heavy weapons. I often saw government forces transporting antiaircraft guns in the back of pickup trucks on Tubman Boulevard. Now they were driving around in my neighborhood with those antiaircraft guns and other heavy weapons. BBC had reported that Charles Taylor's NPFL forces were in Congo Town. Congo Town was the community next to mine; therefore, that meant we were about to be captured by the NPFL rebel forces. Also, my neighborhood was a very strategic area to capture because it included the St. Joseph Catholic Hospital, which was one of the few fully functioning hospitals in Monrovia at the time. Being that this hospital was still under President Doe's controlled territory, it would certainly cripple the government to lose one of its major institutions. Many wished that President Doe could resign and leave office so that the destruction of lives and property could come to an end. However, the reality was that President Doe was too greedy to give up the seat of power. He was known as a strong man. He certainly did not want to have to leave office because of one of his former employees.

As the fighting drew closer, the environment had reached a very high level of tension. I started to hear guns firing more frequently in the Congo Town area. These sounds were so terrifying to me as a child. They were nothing like I had experienced before. The sounds were even more traumatic because it brought about fear, fear of the unknown. The sounds were even more fearful at night. Perhaps it was because I was only a child and children are often afraid of the dark.

The frequency of the gunfire kept increasing, and the sounds kept getting closer. It was very difficult to carry on with the daily activities of life. We were not able to go to the market to get food. In fact, going to the market would have been useless because there was no food available. We were also unable to go out and fetch water. Therefore, we had to ration water so that it could last longer. We used the water that we got from the well to drink. We did not always have clean water to drink. Therefore, we had to boil our water to purify so that we could be able to drink it. We also dug makeshift wells in our yard or wherever we could get water to use. We used the water from the makeshift wells to bath, wash clothing, etc. We learned this method because it was provided by nongovernmental organizations such as Red Cross, United Nations, and Medicine San Frontier. It helped to decrease the outbreak of cholera and dysentery, which was a major problem in Liberia at the time. So many Liberians died of these illnesses during that time.

Sadly, the conditions that we lived in at the time were not fitting for any human to exist in. Unfortunately, pregnant women, elderly people, and young children were placed in such deplorable conditions because of greed and hatred. I witnessed my mother, who was about nine months pregnant, enduring the deplorable conditions that she was placed in as a result of the war. My mother was a very strong woman, and I never saw her complaining. I could see that her life was becoming very difficult. Having now had children of my own and seeing what is required for expecting mothers to properly birth children, it is painful to imagine that my mother had to endure such hardship. This was supposed to be a joyful time in my mother's life. Instead, it became a burdensome time for her.

By the first week of August 1990, my community had become a battlefield. The NPFL forces were now at our front door. I remembered on one hot afternoon, we were on our backyard porch when a man and two women came and asked my parents to use our coal pot stove to cook their food. They told us that they were from the hospital, and they just wanted help preparing their meal. They were all wearing red T-shirt and blue jeans, which was the official uniform for the NPFL rebel forces. However, I believe that we did not think much of the similarity in their clothing to that of the NPFL rebel forces because of the females. Also, it was not unusual for my family to help hospital visitors with food, water, our bathroom, and whatever we could assist with. So we were simply doing what was normal for us. While they were cooking, we started to hear gun firing, and it sounded very close by. It was loud and scary, and we all ran inside our home. My mother told the man and both women to come inside our home. However, they told my mother that they were okay and that we should go ahead. I ran into my parents' room along with my brothers and mother. We all hid, lying on the carpet, and I hid under my parents' bed. The gun firing sounded like it was right in front of our home. The bullets were hitting our home. We could hear the boots of soldiers and metals clinging as they walked in front of our home. I remembered a certain weapon that sounded like a trumpet when it was fired. I believed many referred to it as the dragon. It shook our home when it was fired. Surprisingly, the gunfight was brief. I was expecting a long gunfight, but that did not happen. I believe that the shooting did not even last for an hour. After the fight, it became very quiet. The air seemed still. Nothing moved, and for a while, we stayed inside. We did not know when it was safe to come out. We did not know what was happening. Eventually, my father went out to see what was going on. After assessing the area, he went out and checked on the neighbors. My father later returned and informed us that it was okay to come out. I was skeptical, but I trusted my father. So I came out along with my mother, brothers, and uncle. I expected to see NPFL soldiers walking around. However, I did not see NPFL rebel forces or government forces in our community. We also did not see the man and women who had asked to use our coal pot stove. I wondered briefly what had happened to them. We all concluded that the pair were likely members of Charles Taylor's NPFL forces that were on a reconnaissance mission. I quickly moved on to other concerns as I was anxious about the future of me and my family.

After that incident, my parents thought it wise to start preparing for the unknown. My parents hid whatever valuables that they had such as their wedding rings, my mother's jewelries, and their cash. My brothers and I also packed some clothes in our school backpacks. A few members of the government forces later returned, but they were much fewer than before.

For the next few days, there was strong tension in the air. The fighting had now reached my neighborhood. My community, which I had so many fond memories of, had now become a battlefield. The anticipation of becoming liberated from President Doe's government forces appeared to be getting closer. I was expecting that we would obtain real freedom and that our lives would be so much better. Perhaps we could finally gain access to food, electricity, drinking water, and, most importantly, protection.

A few days after the initial fighting, we heard another gunfight. This time it sounded a little further away from our home. Unfortunately, this time the gunfight occurred at night, and I was very afraid. I recalled hearing lots of small-arms fire. I anticipated that the fighting would reach our front yard like it had previously done. I went to hide under my parents' bed again to hide from the gunfire and the sound of it as well. I did not sleep nor did I want to sleep. I don't believe any of us slept well at all that night. The fighting lasted for several hours although it was not as intense as the previous fight. I remembered that it made for a really long night. The fighting eventually ended in the early morning hours, and I was able to get some sleep on the carpet in my parents' bedroom. Little did we know that the rebel forces had taken control of our community.

The following morning, I woke up to my father instructing me to quickly get my backpack and get out of our home.

Journey of Terror

When we exited our home, we saw many of our neighbors walking toward Tubman Boulevard, which was the major road in that area. We did not know where we would be going, so we simply followed the crowd. We had initially planned to go to my paternal grandmother's farm in Totota. However, there was just a lot of chaos, and understandably, everyone was trying to get out of the danger zone. So we did what everyone was doing. We walked and ran along with hundreds of people, following them to the unknown. As we continued to walk, I also saw a sea of bullet shell casings on the road. They were so many shell casings on the road that I could not see the asphalt. The civilians were walking on both sides of the road, and a few NPFL fighters walked in the middle of the road. As we continued to walk away from our neighborhood, we saw a few SUVs and pickups speeding toward the front lines. There were several soldiers holding on to the vehicle, displaying their RPGs (rocket propelled grenade) or M60 machine guns (commonly referred to as 50 Caliber in Liberia).

Not too long into our journey, things began to become weird. As we were walking, I saw an image that is still burned in my mind today. I saw a man wearing a dress, a wig, and a mask that looked like it was straight out of a horror film. He was carrying a long assault rifle and wearing a pair of boots. He seemed distorted, perhaps intoxicated. He appeared very dangerous, and I became very afraid. Fear overwhelmed me like never before. I felt my knees weakening. It also did not help that he kept saying that he wanted to kill those who were of the Krahn and Mandingo tribes. I also believe that these soldiers were trying to install fear into the hearts and minds of their opponents and also civilians. Fear is a part of the African culture. It also is seen as a sign of power, and it seemed like everyone wanted power. It was not uncommon to see people take drastic measures to get power. Therefore, witchcraft and juju practices were seen as something powerful, and they were widely feared. For those who practiced witchcraft or juju, it provided them with a sense of an advantage. Therefore, it explains why members of the rebel forces turned to the strategy of fear to defeat their opponents. They defeated the government forces soldiers before the battle even began. The strategy of fear worked well for the NPFL forces because they took over most of Liberia from President Doe's forces like wildfire. We used to hear stories of how some members of the NPFL forces would get shot and not be harmed. Some members of the government forces feared the NPFL forces because of the magical powers (juju) that they were believed to have. However, using satanic powers to assist them in doing good probably wasn't the best of ideas. Obviously, nothing good comes out of making a deal with the devil.

Our situation became worse. From the very beginning of our encounter with NPFL forces, they attempted to instill fear in us with mask from horror films and juju powers. Then they were looking to kill people from the Krahn and Mandingo ethnic group. The NPFL rebels were filled with so much hate to the point that they did not portray concern for their own countrymen. Charles Taylor's NPFL forces were causing more harm than they were doing good. They targeted all Liberians except those who were from Nimba County. Even my own family was targeted. This was not because my family was harboring a member of the tribe that was targeted. My family was targeted because both of my parents were government employees. The NPFL soldiers were looking for individuals who worked for the government because they believed that government employees were embezzling government funds. This was far from the truth. My parents struggle to provide for our family because the government under President Doe's regime did not pay its employees in a timely manner. Sometimes, government employees did not get pay for months. This affected every aspect of our lives, including our education. My parents could not always afford to pay our tuition on time, and we had to be kicked out of school several times. So how could my parents now be targeted because of their employment? This was like a double punishment. However, the facts did not matter to them as long as they got to kill more people. NPFL rebels were also checking the legs of men at various checkpoints. They were looking for boot-like marking around the lower legs of men. According to the NPFL rebel forces, this was a sign that you were a soldier because soldiers wore boots. The NPFL rebel forces were searching for boot markings on men's legs because they were trying to determine if members of the government forces were among those trying to flee the battlefield or trying to infiltrate NPFL territory. If anyone was observed with boot markings on their lower leg, they were a candidate to be murdered. During earlier stages of our journey, I saw a military boot in the middle of Tubman Boulevard with a leg sticking out of it. The leg was chopped off at the calf a few inches above the boots. I believe that the boot with the leg was strategically placed to instill fear in us. Unfortunately, many men died innocently because of boot markings. Loggers, security officers, miners, anyone who did work that required them to wear boots to protect their feet faced a likely possibility of being murdered that day.

NPFL rebels were also very interested in taking away what little valuable that we were carrying along that day. Next to looking for Krahn and Mandingo ethnic people to execute, their biggest concern was looking for money and other valuable items to take for themselves. I believe this because the rebels asked more questions about valuables, and they even searched for them at every checkpoint. I believed that there were so many checkpoints because members of the rebel forces wanted more opportunities to violate an already violated people by robbing them of their last valuable items. Everyone in our group was searched multiple times at many checkpoints along the journey. As we stopped at every checkpoint, I noticed that NPFL rebel forces were pulling several individuals aside and conducting further investigations. Many of those who were pulled aside were usually tortured by tying their elbows behind them until they touched or killing them. Charles Taylor rebels referred to tying the elbows as "Tabay." The forms of killings that I observed varied from decapitation, shooting, or hacking. It was terrifying to witness all of these, especially as those victims were crying from the pain that they were suffering. I also saw so many dead bodies lying on the side of the road. Dead bodies were everywhere, and there was a stench everywhere we went. I also saw a few people on the side of the road as we were walking who were not dead yet and were still fighting death. I saw many stray dogs feeding off dead bodies on the side of the road. I could not believe what I was experiencing. My life had gone from a happy and promising life to total anarchy in only a few months. I started to wonder if we were all going to make it alive. At one of the many checkpoints in Congo Town, my family and I were getting harassed and searched when heavy gunfire broke out. I immediately became afraid because I thought that the government forces were launching a counterattack. We were still close to our neighborhood near the German embassy. The rebels told us to run, and we all started running further into rebel-captured territory. Even my mother, who was in her ninth month of pregnancy, had to run for her life carrying whatever belonging that she was able to carry. I don't know how long we ran for, but it was quit challenging carrying those bags while running. I am sure it was even more challenging for my mother. She was in no position to be sprinting at full speed, but she had to do what she had to do to save her life. I will say that she did not hold us back; she kept up with us.

Getting out of the battlefield did not get us out of harm's way. The further we walked into NPFL-captured territories, the more danger we faced. It seemed that danger was becoming our new reality. There was no hope in sight with each moment, with each encounter possibly becoming our last moment before our lives would be taken away. I believe that the many Liberians walking with us felt hopeless. Even members of my own family and household felt hopeless. That is because many of us started to experience high levels of anxiety. We could not see our future. Our only real hope was to flee Liberia and go to a foreign land, where there would be no certainty. When you are in a fire, you jump out. It does not matter where you land. Unfortunately, we also had no means of getting out of Liberia.

We were not close enough to the border towns to cross the border. We continued our journey, not knowing where we were going. My parents' initial plan was to go to my paternal grandmother's farm in Totota, Bong County. It would have been a very long trip to make by foot, and we also did not know if she was still at her farm, or even alive. So we continued to follow the group as they walked, not knowing where we were going.

As we continued the journey, the checkpoints seemed to increase. Each checkpoint created an opportunity for Charles Taylor's rebels to intimidate, torture, steal, or kill another innocent Liberian who was simply seeking protection and safety. The checkpoints were intimidating, with human skulls and often dead bodies with their elbows tied behind their backs while touching would be lying on the ground. The NPFL rebels were very aggressive and cruel to most people. It almost was as if their sole purpose for being there was to steal properties away from the civilian population. Civilians that were caught hiding highly valuable items or large amount of cash were often treated more harshly. Trying to hide your possession from the rebel forces could lead to torture, or even death. The rebel forces often supported their actions with the reasoning that those Liberians who have valuable possessions or large amount of cash were often government employees who were misappropriating government funds. I became very anxious every time I came to a checkpoint because I was carrying a large amount of money in my underwear. Several members of our group were also hiding cash and other valuable jewelries in their underclothes and other parts of our bodies. We were at serious risk of being harmed if those valuables possessions were discovered. It would have also been unfortunate for me and members of our group if the wife of my father's friend was discovered with us. She was a member of the Krahn ethnic group, the sought-after ethnic group. Hiding her was a major offense to members of Charles Taylor's rebel forces. If she was discovered among us, we would have all been likely tortured and eventually murdered. We were all very conscious about what that meant for us.

While I experienced a lot of traumatic events at the many checkpoints that I encountered, the journey itself was a horrific experience.

We came across so many corpses lying around. Many of the corpses that we came across had been lying in the open humid air, with no dignity. Many of those corpses were in a state of decay and smelling awful, I came across an open field in the Paynesville community where a mass murder had occurred. I am not certain which party committed the heinous act, but I lost even more hope seeing all those dead people just lying out there. There were so many of them that I could barely see the grass. I wondered if this was the Duport Road massacre or the Cow Field Massacre as I was not very familiar with the area. Regardless of which massacre it was, it was terrifying to have observed the aftermath. I was grateful that I was not there when the massacre actually occurred.

As we continued our journey, we came upon another massacre scene. This massacre scene was different. We came upon a river that was flowing down to lower grounds. The river was filled with human bodies being carried by the water current. I stood on the lower grounds looking up the river. As I waited to cross the river with my family, all that I could see was dead bodies floating by in the water. I was not sure where the bodies were from. My guess was that another massacre recently occurred in a town up the river and that the dead were dumped into the river. This massacre had noticeably more dead bodies than the other massacres that I had just encountered. I remembered this scene so well because I had to cross the river while getting around so many dead bodies. I had such a difficult time getting across the river because the water was just below my mouth. Also, I was carrying bags with me, which made it difficult to balance in the water. My younger brother was not tall enough to make it across the river, so my uncle carried him on his shoulder. As I crossed the river, I kept getting struck by dead bodies floating across the river. The bodies were heavy and almost knocked me over. I was afraid while crossing the river because of the current of the river. Also, I was afraid to be swept by the current because I could not swim. My mother also managed to cross the river despite her conditions. She was enduring so many challenges, but she had to keep walking along with us. There was no opportunity for her to rest, and the rebels kept pushing us to keep moving. Also no one wanted to get the attention of the members of NPFL rebels because encounter with them would likely lead to a very bad experience.

As we continued to walk to our unknown destination, we had a brief opportunity for my mother to rest. I do not recall what lead to us getting the opportunity to get rest, but I do recall that my mother and I got the opportunity to sit on a gallon used to carry water. Unfortunately, even during that brief period of resting, traumatic experiences still haunted us. As my mother and I were sitting and getting much needed rest, we observed a man been pushed to the side of the road by NPFL rebels. My mother, sensing that the NPFL rebels were about to torture or murder the man, got up and told me to follow her. She was trying to protect me from witnessing another traumatic event or getting injured. As we walked away from the scene, I heard the man pleading with the rebels. I can still remember that scene today. He was a dark-skinned man with a full beard. He was also slim built. The man had been stripped down to his underpants. As the man was pleading with the rebels, he was shot right before our eyes. The man struggled in the grass after he was shot. I felt so afraid because I was right there. I could only hope that me, members of my family, and those travelling with us would not be next. My mother quickly took me away, and we joined the rest of the party to continue our journey.

Fear Becomes Reality

As we continued our journey, there were other challenges that we experienced within our group. Those challenges, as traumatic as they were, seemed to be the norm on that day. Most of those who were travelling also experienced similar things. The conditions on that day were very extreme. Like many others, we had been walking since approximately 6:00 a.m., and by noon, none of us had rested or had a drink of water or food to eat. Water and food were luxury, and they were simply not available. I can't imagine how difficult it was for my mother to endure those challenges considering that she was in her third trimester. During a period of her pregnancy, when she would have likely been resting herself and staying off her feet, she was hiking miles under extreme circumstances. As harsh as those conditions were, it was consumed by the extreme and imminent danger that we faced from the NPFL rebel forces. That was a very long day, and it seemed like the day would never end. All day long we did our best to evade encountering NPFL rebel members and their supporters. Unfortunately, we could not avoid sights of deceased bodies, murders, tortures, and other sights of atrocities that were committed right before us. Even worse were the continuous dreaded visits to the various checkpoints where we always ran the risk of facing some real danger. I'm sure that other Liberians also felt the same about those checkpoints. Majority of the checkpoints seemed to be manned by angry soldiers who were always looking for opportunities to rob, torture, and murder innocent Liberians, who they claimed to be liberating. I saw so many people killed, mercilessly beaten, and dehumanized that it began to become normal for me to witness such atrocities.

Even the sound of gun firing, which petrified me in the early stages of the war, started to become normal to me. At some point, I only became concern with the sound of gunfire because I wanted to learn if I was the intended target. If I could not determine if I was the target, I continued minding my business. There was also the danger of been struck by stray bullets. Stray bullets were everywhere, and they were often heard flying in the air. The whistling of stray bullet was something that I could never get used to because it meant imminent harm was very likely. I could not see them, but I could hear them very well. This was one of those things that really increased my anxiety. Every time I heard the whistle of a stray bullet, my heart felt like it would explore out of my chest because I feared that I would get killed or badly injured. After all, I knew of many incidents where random citizens died or got serious injuries from the stray bullets.

We continued on the horrific journey until we came to another checkpoint on the Monrovia-Kakata Highway. Unlike the other checkpoints that we had encountered, this one was different. At this checkpoint, males and females were separated. Males and females went to different checkpoints. Therefore, in my group, all of the males, which included my father, my father's friend and his nephew, my uncle, both of my brothers and I, went into the building where all the males went. At this checkpoint, the rebels were even more aggressive. They were drastically interrogating most of us in the building that was used as a checkpoint. Charles Taylor's NPFL rebels were conducting thorough investigations to locate members of the Krahn and Mandingo ethnic group. The rebels were also looking for members of the government force that were trying to escape or might be trying to infiltrate NPFL-held territories. So many individuals were tortured and murdered at this checkpoint. The dreadful cry by grown men for their lives was more frequent at this checkpoint. Too often many of those dreadful cries were followed by the sound of gun firing. No one had to tell anyone what that meant. I, like many others, had witnessed firsthand the killing of many people in similar situations. I recall that the rooms were dark because of the lack of electricity, which made the environment even scarier. The rebels were also searching bags and even underclothing for valuables such as jewelries and cash. If you were discovered hiding your valuable items, you would likely be punished by torture or sometimes even death. I was very afraid because my father had given me a bundle of cash to hide in my underpants. Fortunately for me, I was not thoroughly searched. After everyone in my travel party was searched, we walked out of that dark building into the light.

After exiting the checkpoint, we gathered together and waited for the females in our party. My father's friend's wife and two daughters eventually came out but without my mother. I wasn't initially concerned about my mother because I simply thought that she separated herself from my father's friend's wife because she was being sought after by members of Charles Taylor's NPFL. After waiting for several minutes, I became concerned. We all did because we started asking about her. My father asked his friend's wife if she saw my mother. She told us that she was not with my mother when she was being checked. Although it was a great risk, my father decided to go back to the females-only checkpoint to check on my mother's well-being. My father did not make it very far. One of the female soldiers turned him back and told him that only females were allowed at the checkpoint. My father not wanting to attract negative attention turned around and left the location. We figured that it would be safe to wait for her instead of risking him being tortured or killed. We patiently waited for several more minutes, but soon it became clear to us that something was wrong. We had waited long enough for those walking behind us to clear the checkpoint and walk out of our sight. My father, in a state of desperation, made another attempt to go back to the females-only checkpoint and ask about my mother. This time I was afraid for my father. I had seen members of Charles Taylor's rebel forces torture and kill people for very minimum reasons, and I believe that they wouldn't hold back on anyone who disobeyed their directions. I was also concerned about my brothers and me because we had just been disconnected from my mother. Losing my father would have caused us to become orphans and be left in the care of my uncle Nana, who was himself only a teenager. The rebels again stopped my father and started to threaten him, even as he tried to explain that he came back because his pregnant wife was still at the checkpoint. When the female soldiers started yelling at my father, I thought he was done. I believed that the rebels were going to kill him. Even worse, the noise from the female rebels attracted the male rebels. One of the male rebels started to approach my father. The male rebel first threatened to take my father away. By the grace of God, the male soldier changed his mind. He told my father to return to us, and that if he came back to the checkpoint, he would be killed. My father returned to us without our mother. He was very disappointed. We all were. I understand that it was a very difficult time for him. He had just lost his high-school sweetheart, and he could do nothing about it. I know that it was even more difficult for him as an individual because he is a strong-minded person. He normally would not have accepted a denial regarding looking for my mother. I believe that he only did so because he knew that if he persisted, he would be killed and he did not want to leave us as orphans. I appreciated him making decisions that would have led to my brothers and me not becoming orphans. I can't say that we would have survived today without him. If we weren't killed, we could have likely been taken and turned into child soldiers. I saw so many child soldiers, some even younger than me. The rifles that they carried were even longer than them. They often appeared to be in a daze, maybe from intoxication. They were often used as killing machines to torture and kill innocent civilians. I certainly did not want to be manipulated in this way. That is why I'm so thankful that my father made the wise decision to return to us and not force the issue at the females-only checkpoint. I cannot and will never understand how this experience affected my father. He met my mother in high school when he attended Booker Washington Institute. Through the years, they had built a family together. Now she was suddenly taken away from him with no closure.

We picked up our belongings and continued our journey. I was hopeful that we might see her and reconnect with her. As we continue our journey, my younger brother told us that he had seen our mother in the back of a truck that had just driven past us. I also saw the truck, but it was now a little further away from our group. My younger brother said that our mother waved at us. I did not see her, but I believe my brother. Although he was young, he was old enough to recognize her. If she was in the truck, we wondered where she would be going. If she followed our original plan and went to my paternal grandmother's home, there was no guarantee that she would still be there. Many people had fled their homes, and we had no way of knowing if she would be there. Also, how would we be able to get to my paternal grandmother's home? We were travelling by foot, and it would have taken forever for us to get there. The situation in Liberia at the time was very chaotic, and even the best of plans would be very difficult to implement.

As we continued on our journey, we later caught up with my father's friend and his family. We updated them with the information that we had gotten disconnected from our mother. It was a very tough day for everyone. Besides the fact that my family lost my mother, my father's friend was still dealing with the challenge of trying to hide his wife. Not only that, but my father's friend also had two young daughters that they had to make the journey with. While one of the girls was an infant and was transported on the back of her mother, the other daughter, approximately four years old, made most of the journey on foot. I'm not sure how she did it, especially with very minimum food, water, or rest. I believe that God strengthened her to do what she needed to do. Although she was very young, it would have been almost impossible for anyone to carry her while carrying other large bags. We had to continue our journey so that we could get to our final destination before dark.

It was evening, and the darkness of the night was almost upon us. I did not know where we were going but I knew that it would not be a good idea for us to be travelling at night. With as much terror that I encountered that day, I certainly did not want to encounter even more terror under the darkness of the night when things often got really bad. My father, recognizing the danger of travelling at night, told us to pick up the pace. We did the best that we could, but the many checkpoints greatly delayed us in our travels.

During our travels, we continued to experience many close calls on our lives. I remembered one in particular. I believe that I still hold this encounter in my memory because of all of the close calls that we had, I really did believe that this was one of the times that something bad was really going to happen. That evening we came upon a checkpoint where one of the soldiers believed that my father had money hidden in his belonging. Although he searched our properties, he for some reason believed that my father had money. I could only guess that was because my father was plump. To many members of the rebel forces and culturally, being plump was a sign of wealth. So the soldier presented himself as someone who wanted to help my father. He told my father that he wanted to help him by taking us through a shorter route. My father, sensing something wrong, told the soldier that he was okay and that he would like to continue to the route that everyone was taking. However, the soldier kept insisting that my father take this route through the bushes. My father also continued to insist that he wanted to stay on the route that he was already on. Realizing that the soldier would eventually get his way since he was the one in the position of authority, my father had to think quickly. While my father was speaking with the soldier, he began to fake a medical emergency. My father started to behave as if he was experiencing shortness of breath. My father even went down to the ground to create the appearance that he was losing consciousness. The soldier, to my surprise, started to show some concern. He quickly left to go and get water for my father. After the soldier was out of our sight, my father got up and told us to quickly get our belonging and leave that area. My father told us that he believed that the soldier was attempting to take us through the bush route because he wanted to murder us and take our possessions. As we were leaving the checkpoint, I was very concerned because I feared that the soldier would be very angry upon his return and hunt us down. If that soldier had found us, it could have been big trouble for us. I prayed that the soldier did not come after us or, even worse, find us. We walked very quickly without looking like we were running away from one of the soldiers. As God would have it, we were able to get away from that situation and continue our journey—a journey of terror that couldn't seem to come to an end. I recall that as a child, I could usually look up at the beautiful sky and find hope in challenging situations. On this day, no matter how many times I looked up, I just could not seem to find any bit of hope. It just seemed like a bad dream with no sense of hope in sight.

The number of atrocious events that I had experienced on that day had taken every bit of hope that I had out of me. Fortunately, my father continued to lead us in our journey. In spite of all the danger that we were encountering, he continued to lead us with wisdom and bravery. Another event that I remember occurred when we arrived in another checkpoint. While standing at this checkpoint waiting to be checked, some of the soldiers started to give us a difficult time. I thought that this could be the moment that I did not want to think about. These guys seemed to have made up their minds about us. Then I saw a soldier who was standing at the checkpoint. He appeared to be someone who had some influence among the other soldiers. He had two belts of bullets crisscrossed on his chest like an action figure. He was also carrying an M60 machine gun. Usually, I would have been impressed by this soldier; however, this time around I was not. This was because of the many negative experiences that I had that day from members of Charles Taylor's NPFL forces. Actually, I was very intimidated by this soldier because I did not know if he wanted to kill me. As I was worrying about the possibility of it being our last checkpoint before we were tortured or murdered, my father spoke to the soldier with the large machine gun. Then my father stated that he knew the soldier from years back and started to make references to some of the places that they might have known each other from. The countenance of the mean-looking soldier suddenly changed for the better. He looked excited. I thought that maybe my father really did know this soldier. The soldier made the other soldiers who were harassing us to stop and leave us alone. In fact, he made the other soldiers give us water to drink. This was very helpful since water was not available to us during our journey. After drinking, my father extended thanks to the soldier, and we continued our journey. Little did I know that my father did not actually know the soldier. My father later informed me that he only acted like he knew the soldier because he felt that the soldiers at that checkpoint had already made up their minds to kill us. My father also informed me that the soldier had offered to have us transported. My father admitted that he declined the offer because he did not want the soldier to realize that he had tricked him.

The end result was good for us obviously. However, I believe that it was God who made his bravery to have a successful result. The reality is that if my father was found to have been lying, we could have likely been tortured and killed.

Shortly after this encounter, we came to our final destination. We did not know that this was where we were going, but it ended up being the same location where my father's college graduation was held. We arrived at the University of Liberia Fendall Campus in the late evening. The campus had been turned into a displacement camp. I still remember the location from the attendance of my father's graduation ceremony. It was so beautiful then. Now the scene was different. It was crowded and without electricity. Our initial experience was pretty chaotic. We did not know where to go, what to do, or where we would be staying. We did not know how long we would be staying at Fendall Campus. To make matters worse, there were still soldiers intimidating members of the public. These soldiers were taking advantage of already disadvantaged people in a desperate situation. Even after reaching our final destination, members of the NPFL were still robbing citizens of whatever little value they possessed. These soldiers were also continuing to investigate and accuse individuals of being members of the Armed Forces of Liberia and also members of the Krahn and Mandingo ethnic groups. It seemed like our new location would be an extension of the journey that we had just made. I asked myself, how long could we exist in such environment? There were too many things going on that day that could not be resolved. I was exhausted, and I knew that worrying could not solve my concerns.

My family eventually found a space on the floor that we could sleep on. We were lucky I guess because there was lack of floor space available for the thousands of displaced Liberians that were taking refuge at the Fendall Campus. I lay down on the solid tile floor to finally get some rest. After all, it had been a very rough and long day. A day without much food or water. A day without being able to conduct personal hygiene. A day of walking all day long in the hot humid sun and rain as well. A day of watching so many tortures and murders. Most significantly, a day that my mother, who was nine months pregnant, was snatched away from us without us knowing what became of her. In spite of all the negatives that we encountered, I was able to experience a light moment that day. At the end of the day, as we approached the Fendall Campus, it started to become dark. As night fell upon us, I observed lights flickering in the dark. It was very beautiful. I had never seen anything like this before. I later learned that those lights were from fireflies. My parents did not allow us to stay out at night; therefore, I did not have the opportunity to experience fireflies. My experience of the beautiful light display from the fireflies enlightened my day. I guess I was looking for something positive after a very negative day, and this light show was just the thing that did it for me.

Fendall Displacement Camp

The night of my arrival at Fendall displacement camp was a very challenging time. When my family, friends, and I arrived that evening, it was very dark, and it seemed like thousands of people were in a hurry for various reasons. Those who were already established at the displacement camp were in a hurry to settle in for the night. Those of us who had just arrived were in a hurry to find a spot on the floor large enough to establish a new residence and settle in for the night. My father eventually connected with the local leader of those staying at the displacement camp. This gentleman happened to be a pastor. He was able to assist us, and we were able to find a spot to settle down on. Our small space on the solid tile flooring was sectioned off by two office tables positioned in an *L* form to provide privacy. While we did our best to create some privacy, there was not enough opportunity to be private. We shared the room with many other families. There were infants and toddlers crying everywhere. It was very loud although it was late. We settled our newly modified family of now five for the night. My father's friend and his family were also fortunate to get a spot next to ours on the floor. The floors were very solid and uncomfortable. Fortunately, we made it to the end of the day. A very exhaustive day. A day filled with so many negative experiences that I could never forget. Fatigue won, and my eyes started to get heavy. I eventually fell asleep. My experience from August 10, 1990, will forever haunt me.

The next morning, we all woke up in a strange environment. We were not familiar with the environment that we now found ourselves in. We did not know where to get items from. We did not know where to go and get a bath or use the toilet. We did not know where to go to get food. There were no stores opened. There was no electricity or running water. Most concerning was the fact that we were about to be governed by the same soldiers who had been attempting to murder us and rob us of whatever little valuable that we had left. The thought of individuals, who I had witnessed committing horrific acts of atrocities against Liberians, providing care and support for those same Liberians was concerning. At the time, I believed that we did not have a very promising future. The best description of my experience at the Fendall displacement camp was fearful. Besides the previous experiences that I encountered on my journey to Fendall displacement camp, I was now faced with the uncertainty of an unfavorable future. I could not help but wonder what would become of my family and me if we continued to be left in the hands of evil soldiers. It did not help that members of Charles Taylor's NPFL continued to brutalize and murder members of the public as we sought refuge at Fendall displacement camp.

During our first few days at Fendall displacement camp, we played it safe and stayed inside our room because of our fear of being abuse by the soldiers. However, life continued, and we had to go out eventually for various reasons such as finding food and using the bathroom. Also, my father was still desperately trying to locate my mother whose whereabouts was still unknown. My father went out to find help. He solicited the assistance of anyone who he believed could have helped him. He located organizations such as the United Nations (UN), Medicine San Frontier (MSF), and any individual or organizations that he could find to assist him in finding my mother. All of my father's efforts were unsuccessful. Because of the chaos that we were living in and the lack of information that existed at the time, there was no documentation available that we could use in tracking my mother.

My personal living experience on Fendall displacement camp was initially unbearable. I did not want to be there, and I thought that I could not survive in such environment. What really disturbed me was the frequent gunfire that occurred all throughout the day. When these shooting occurred, stray bullets often flew all around. I had the unfortunate experience of having some of those stray bullet fly close by me on Fendall Campus. I was very aware of what could have happened to me if I became struck by one of those bullets. After all, I had witnessed so many people become injured and murdered, and I was very familiar with the damage that a bullet can cause. So you can see why I was so afraid to go outside. During these incidents, I felt like a target being shot at by a blind man. I could have gotten struck by a bullet at any time, and I could have been severely injured or lose my life. For this reason, I stayed inside most of the time upon my arrival at the Fendall displacement camp. However, life continued, and I had to make the difficult decision to go out of my comfort zone and live life. I had to go and use the bathroom, as there were no working bathrooms in the building that I was staying in.

I got to encounter the unfortunate experience of using the toilet at Fendall displacement camp. The toilet at Fendall displacement camp was a large open area with feces everywhere. The smell was horrible, and I could not evade the smell. Even more horrific was that I had to hop over feces to find a clear spot to defecate. To make matters even worse, I had to worry about members of Charles Taylor's rebel forces shooting randomly outdoors as they usually do. The bullets from there gunfire was so close that I could hear the bullets whistling by me as I was defecating. I guess the fear of becoming harmed by the bullets created a distraction from the gross scene that was surrounding me. Initially, I was very afraid of the possibility of been struck by one of those random bullets flying indiscriminately around me. As time went by, this experience became more normal. I could only be afraid for my safety for so long. I believe that I got to the point where I decided to no longer live my life at that level of fear. It was not sustainable because I could not function. I believe that I simply stopped caring about what would happen to me. There was so much harm and disaster going on around me that I figure that sooner or later I would be harmed or killed anyway. I decided to simply live my life as if it was my last. I had totally given up on hope. This was not too hard to understand given the situation around me. Daily, I was witnessing people being murdered and traumatized in the most horrendous way.

Because of the poor living conditions at the displacement camp, an epidemic broke out, which added more challenge to the already wretched conditions at the Fendall displacement camp. Poor sanitation and large amount of people living in close proximity created the opportunity for diseases to spread. The lack of clean drinking water created an outbreak of cholera and dysentery in the camp. Unlike my first experience with the outbreak of the epidemic back in my community, this time I was living in conditions that could result in my family and me contracting the illness. I was no longer safe, and my father could no longer protect my brothers and me like he used to do.

The situation was out of control. Everything was out of our control. Like the previous epidemic outbreak at the Catholic hospital community, so many people died. People were dying from the cholera and dysentery outbreak throughout the camp, especially the young children. Quite often you would hear cries of love ones grieving over the loss of a family member or relative. Mothers were crying over the loss of their babies, fathers were crying over the loss their children, and wives were crying for their husbands. Deaths were happening everywhere around me, even in my room. It was so painful to see the mothers crying that I could almost feel their pain through their weeping.

We did our best to exercise caution and avoid getting ill. We boiled our drinking water before drinking. However, all our efforts did not keep us away from experiencing the infection. The outbreak eventually reached my family. My father became very ill with a cholera infection. He was so ill that he could not sit up or support himself in any way. Of course, I became very concerned because he was the only parent that my brothers and I had left. I did not want to even imagine being without my father, not in those circumstances. My fear of losing my father was made even worse by what I was observing around me. Based on my experience, it appeared that those individuals who contracted cholera or dysentery often died. Now I was concerned that my father's chance of survival was slim to none. The statistics were not in his favor. His appearance worsened as the days went by. He had lost so much weight that he looked like a skeleton.

Even the life in his eyes was fading away. I can best describe my father as someone who was in the process of losing his life. My father could not retain food or water. He excreted every bit of food that he ate. The limited medication that my father's friend and others were able to get my father did not seem to be helping to improve his condition.

As my father's condition declined, I faced the reality that my siblings and I were about to become orphans in a devastating environment. My future and that of my siblings did not look great. In fact, it appeared that our future had just taken a turn for the worse. My brothers and I were without our mother, and now, we faced the possibility of losing the only parent that we had. The situation was more than I could bear. I was only an eleven-year-old child. What could I do to deal with the challenges that I was facing? In that desperate situation, I called out to the only one that I believed could help me. I turned to the God that my mother taught me about. The God that I learned about in Sunday school. The God who could protect me and hear me when I call out to him. For I had no one else who could help me in that situation. When all hope seemed lost and it appeared as if we were all simply awaiting my father's death, God heard my prayers. God answered my prayer through the wife of a Liberian National Police executive member, Col. Albert Moore. Colonel Moore was also one of those individuals that was in fear of his life because he would definitely become a high value target if members of Charles Taylor's rebel forces learned of his rank in the police department. Therefore, he stayed away from the public as much as he possibly could to preserve his life. He only kept close to very few families, and my family happened to be one of them. When the wife of Colonel Moore heard about my father's illness, she made it known that she had a remedy that she believed could cure his illness. She discovered that a mixture of lime and salt could stop my father from excreting. This would be good for my father because he would now be able to retain food and water. Retaining food and water would help my father get the nutrients that his body needed to get stronger and healthier. However, there was one big challenge: there were no limes available in the market. This was prohibited from being sold by members of the rebel forces because they believed that lime had the ability to destroy the power of their "juju" (black magic). If anyone dared to possess lime, they ran the risk of being brutally beaten or even murdered. But by the grace of God, we were able to get our hands on some lime, and she prepared the remedy for my father. We all had our hopes on the remedy and that it would work, and it did work. My father eventually decreased the frequency of excrement. He started to retain his food and water. Fortunately, my father regained his health. We were all relieved that my father regained his health. It was a very narrow escape. So many people died from those illnesses, and it was only God who protected my father during his time of illness.

Meet the General

After my father regained his health, I was able to stop worrying about becoming an orphan. After all, I was only one parent away from becoming an orphan. My family started to learn our way around the Fendall displacement camp. I also wanted to learn my way around and learn where to get daily necessities. Many of those living on the displacement camp also began to venture out more to also find daily necessities. We also came together more to support each other. After all, we only had each other. We were all going through similar situations, and I believe that our similar challenges brought us together. Many of those on the displacement camp turned to God for strength and protection. My father, our family, and the family that we hosted also turned to God. We started to gather in groups to have devotion during the week. This was a time of singing praises to God and thanking God for his blessings in spite of the many challenges that we were facing. This was the real life interpretation of 1 Thessalonians 5:18, "Give thanks in all circumstances, for this is the will for God in Christ Jesus for you." The devotion was led by Bishop Reeves, who was our group leader. I remembered that the devotion times were the most peaceful times that I experienced during my time at Fendall displacement camp. Devotion time allowed me to escape the emotional trauma, chaos, and dangers of everyday life on the displacement camp. God had to be my source of hope and strength because God was the only one who could carry me through the hell that I was currently living in. I was reminded daily about the hell that I was living in. I experienced hell all around me. I saw members of the public beaten mercilessly or killed often by members of Charles Taylor's rebel forces. Members of the Krahn and Mandingo tribes were still sought after to be murder by Charles Taylor's rebels. Therefore, my family continued to exist in the displacement camp with greater risk than others because we were hosting a member of the Krahn ethnic group. Although I was a young boy, I clearly understood that outing this individual would likely lead to the torture and murder of every member of our group. We also faced danger from numerous stray bullets flying around as a result of soldiers shooting randomly. In fact, every time we stepped out of our room, we faced danger as we encountered Charles Taylor's rebels. We could be stopped, interrogated, and searched for no good reason. During these encounters, one would be more concerned about making it through those encounters, alive instead of worrying about their rights being violated. For this reason, I did my best to avoid going out and encountering members of Charles Taylor's rebel forces, especially, the child soldiers. In spite of the danger that we all faced, we still had to go out of our rooms to conduct daily life activities such as doing laundry, going to the market, etc. Life goes on, as they say.

One day I decided to go outside to ease myself and take a bath at one of the local creeks. We did not take baths often because we were afraid to go out for fear of encountering Charles Taylor's rebel forces. On this day, I felt really dirty, and I really needed to take a bath. So I went out to the creek without telling my dad, Uncle Nana, or anyone. This I must admit was not a good idea. If anything had happened to me, no one would know of my whereabouts. This was obviously a very foolish decision that I can only attribute to my age as a preteen and my very independent personality. As I was walking to the creek, I noticed several people cleaning the side of the road. The roads had become dirty because of members of the public dropping sugarcane peelings on the side of the road when eating sugarcane. Unaware, I had walked into a mandatory cleanup campaign held by Charles Taylor's rebels. Charles Taylor rebels were forcing every member of the public who was outside at the time to stop whatever they were doing and clean up the roads. I did not know what was going on; therefore, I continued to walk to the creek for my bath. I thought that those who were cleaning were volunteering to clean up.

As I was walking, a car suddenly stopped right next to me. A man started screaming insults at me and asked me why I was not cleaning like everyone else. I did not know who this man was, but I knew that only Charles Taylor rebels had access to vehicles. Therefore, I knew that he was a member of Charles Taylor's rebel forces. This man also appeared to be a high-ranking officer because I noticed that he had bodyguards with him. This high-ranking officer was apparently very upset at me, and I didn't know what to do with myself. I was afraid, and I did not know what to say. How could I respond to this man in the right way? I was even more afraid because this was the first time that I had had a negative encounter with one of Charles Taylor's rebel without my father there to guide or protect me. At this moment, I greatly regretted my decision to go out and explore my independence without letting anyone know of my whereabouts. As this high-ranking rebel officer continued to berate me, a transmission came across his handheld radio. Whatever was transmitted on his radio must have been really important because he stopped berating me. He yelled at me and ordered me to start cleaning. As he was leaving, he yelled, "I will be right back." After the encounter, another member of Charles Taylor's rebel force, who was on the scene and had witnessed what had occurred, approached me. He asked me if I knew who the man was that I had just encountered. I was afraid, so I did not respond to the soldier. The soldier then stated that the man who I had just encountered was Isaac Musa, Gen. Isaac Musa. He did not need to say more, Gen. Isaac Musa was known to be one of Charles Taylor's most-feared generals. Gen. Isaac Musa was known for committing so many atrocities around Liberia, and he was feared by all. I became even more afraid when I learned that I was that close to such a deadly and wicked person. Not too long into my cleaning, the same soldier who confirmed that I had encountered Gen. Isaac Musa came back to me. He stated that I was not going to be done when Gen. Isaac Musa returned. The soldier told me that if the general came back and saw me, he was likely going to kill me. Therefore, he told me to get out of the area. I was only a child and very unfamiliar with Fendall Campus. I did not know where to go, and I feared that if I ran into the general again, he would be really upset and likely kill me. However, God must have spoken to that soldier on that day. The soldier told a few others and me to follow him into the bushes. I did not know where we were going. Scary as it was to be following a member of Charles Taylor's rebel forces, who were known murderers, into the bushes, I still followed him. After all, I really did not have a choice. He took us to a large bush with large trees, and he pointed his hand forward and told us to run in the direction that he was pointing to. As we all entered the bushes, trying to find our way through the dense bushes, we started to hear gun firing. At first, I thought that the shooting was from someplace else. It was common to hear small-arms fire as Charles Taylor's rebels were known to shoot their assault rifle sporadically. I quickly realized that we were the target after I started hearing the sound of bullets whizzing by me. I heard a few bullets strike trees next to me as I was running away from the gunfire. As the shooting was going on, I was running so fast that I could not feel my foot touch the ground. I continued running, not knowing where I was going until we all came to an opening. When we got to the opening, I saw the marketplace where we often went to buy food items. I breathed a sigh of relief because I was able to recognize where I was. I made my way back to my room thinking about how much trouble I could have caused my father and family. The guilt haunted me for several weeks after that incident. It had to be one of the worst mistakes that I have ever committed. So many negative results could have come out of my foolish decision to go out alone without informing anyone about where I was going. I could have been murdered, taken into custody by Charles Taylor's rebels and turned into a child soldiers, etc. Nevertheless, by the grace of God, none of those horrible things happened to me. I could not have imagined the pain that I could have cost my father especially after he had just experienced being separated from his wife. I was really grateful to God in that moment that I did not cause my father to relive the experience of losing another family member. I definitely learned my lesson that day. That mistake I promised not to make again in my life.

The Death of President Doe

I continued to deal with life on Fendall displacement camp, this time being as cautious as I could be. As impossible as it might sound, I experienced a few fun moments at Fendall displacement camp. At the camp, I was able to experience things such as going to the creek to take bath. My father was very strict, and he did not allow my brothers and me the opportunity to explore the natural living conditions that my peers had access to. They basically kept us away from anything that they believe was dangerous for us. So whenever we ventured outside, it was a very exciting time for my brothers and me. We usually went to the creek to do laundry and take a bath. Of course, privacy meant nothing during that time. There were usually others at the creek doing laundry or taking a bath. These moments of excitement and fun were often short lived. The reality of the brutal life that I was experiencing was all too overwhelming to escape from. Life on Fendall displacement camp was filled with so many negatives. Just about every day someone would die from an illness. It was not unusual for the individuals at the displacement camp to be brutally beaten or murdered, often for minimal reasons. The experience of hunger was felt by almost everyone on the camp. What made matters worse was that there appeared to be no end to the nightmare that we were living in. President Doe and his government forces were still being stubborn and digging their heels in, refusing to leave office. In spite of the suffering of the Liberian people and the destruction of the nation, President Doe seemed to have made up his mind about staying in power as the president of Liberia. Charles Taylor's forces were in Monrovia, but they were not advancing as they previously did. They had been stopped, and they were battling President Doe's government forces. Also in the mix was another warring faction, which was formerly a part of Charles Taylor's National Patriotic Front of Liberia. This new warring faction would be called Independent National Patriotic Front of Liberia, and it was headed by Gen. Prince Johnson. Therefore, these three groups were all fighting against one another at the same time. I, like most people, were confused about what was going to happen to us. The future was very uncertain. However, we got a bit of good news on the radio while listening to BBC. As usual, I was able to listen to the news when my father and the adults in my surrounding were listening to the radio. One day I was listening to BBC when I learned that a group called ECOWAS (Economic Community of West African States) was sending peacekeepers called ECOMOG (Economic Community of West African Monitoring Group) to stabilize Liberia and stop the fighting. ECOMOG was a multinational military organization consisting of nations from ECOWAS. The ECOWAS nations all consisted of nations from within West Africa. This exciting news was quickly drowned by news of Charles Taylor's refusal to allow ECOMOG peacekeepers into Liberia. Charles Taylor vowed to fight the peacekeepers if they attempt to come unto the shores of Liberia. News of Charles Taylor's refusal to allow the peacekeepers into Liberia was very depressing to me. Charles Taylor's refusal to allow peacekeepers into Liberia meant more suffering, more hunger, more murders, and more negativity from Charles Taylor's leadership. News of Charles Taylor's refusal to allow ECOMOG peacekeepers into Liberia was a dream killer for me, and I am sure for many others as well. My hopes and dreams of getting from under the rulership of Charles Taylor seemed to be slipping away. Hopes and dreams always seemed to be killed under Charles Taylor's authority. So many successful peace agreements had been reversed by Charles Taylor, which only prolonged the war. A war that continued to result in more deaths and destructions in Liberia. Fortunately, I learned from BBC that Gen. Prince Johnson and his INPFL rebel forces volunteered to protect the peacekeepers and allow them to access the Liberian shores. The INPFL forces were able to successfully grant the peacekeepers access to Liberia.

In the month of September, we were all going about our lives as we normally did on the Fendall displacement camp. Everything seemed normal. We were all dealing with the challenges of living on the displacement camp. By the early evenings, we started to observe lots of activities from Charles Taylor's rebel forces. They were excited, and their vehicles were speeding up and down the road with more frequency than usual. They would occasionally fire a few rounds into the air. I was not sure if they were trying to intimidate the public as they so often do or if they were celebrating some good news. I did notice that this time around, they were shooting more than they usually did. Their actions created a real concern for me. I did not know what was going on. Nobody did. So naturally, I became fearful. My fear was that a battle had started. After all, Charles Taylor's forces also had to be concerned about attacks from Gen. Prince Johnson's rebel forces (INPFL).

Just before 5:00 p.m., the adults gathered around the radio to listen to the news as they often do. We kids also gathered around the adults to listen to the news as well. All of us children would often take our place outside of the circle that the adults had formed. Although we were very young, we came to learn the importance of listening to the news. After all, we were all impacted by the war. The information that we learned from the news was either helpful or hurtful. Either way, we were at least informed about what was going on, and it often helped us in our daily decision-making. However, we were only children, and we followed the direction of our parents. Although we were children, we would often decide not to complain to our parents or give them a difficult time about wanting things, even if we had legitimate needs for these items. We did not want to be a burden to our father because we knew what situation we were living in. My brothers and I certainly understood that my father was very limited under the current circumstances that we were in. So, my brothers and I made it a point to not complain about hunger, illnesses, and other challenges that we encountered. We also understood that our father was dealing with a mountain of challenges. My father had just lost contact with his wife and mother of his children. He had also just endured cholera, which almost cost him his life. He had enough on his plate, and my brothers and I did all that we could to ease the tension in his life.

At 5:00 p.m., the theme song for the 5:00 p.m. evening news started. It is a sound that is still familiar to me, and I am sure many others who lived in that era in Liberia. I do not believe that this theme song will ever leave my memory. The familiar voice of Elizabeth Blunt came on the radio. We all listened carefully to learn what the increase in activities were all about. As I recall, the news that evening had to be the most important news of that period in Liberia. The news reporter on *BBC News* reported that President Samuel Kanyon Doe, head of state of the Republic of Liberia had been captured by Gen. Prince Johnson and his INPFL forces. It seemed unreal that President Doe, who appeared to be untouchable, could be captured by anyone, least a small rebel group such as the INPFL. Charles Taylor's rebels were certainly excited. After all, their main goal was to remove President Doe from his presidential position. I also observed that many of those listening to the news were also relieved and excited that President Doe had been captured. After all, he was the source of the affliction and torment that the people of Liberia were experiencing. His refusal to give up power lead to a fight that destroyed many lives and properties in Liberia. I, like many other Liberians, later learned that President Doe was brutally tortured and killed by members of the INPFL. Many seem to believe that President Doe deserved his fate. I heard many making the statement that "If you live by the sword, you will die by the sword," referencing Matthew 26:52 (ESV). I did not fully understand the statement at the time.

I was very young when President Doe came to power. I later learned of the brutal coup that President Doe led, which enabled him to become the president of Liberia. On the journey to becoming president of Liberia, President Doe murdered and caused the execution of many Liberians. I personally do not believe that General Johnson torturing of President Doe was the best way to punish the president. However, like the saying goes, "Evil begets evil."

Shortly after President Doe was captured and murdered, there were rumors of members of the government forces going out and burning down the city of Monrovia in retaliation of President Doe's murder. This cause more anxiety. Many of us in the Fendall displacement camp began to wonder what would be next for us. By this time, we all rightly assumed that more lives and properties were going to be destroyed during this period of retaliation. Yet another thing to add to the many concerns that we already had. I knew and I believed that we could only depend on God for his divine protection. It seemed like we simply had no foreseeable means out of a dire situation.

INPFL Captures Fendall
Displacement Camp

Now that President Doe had been captured and killed, I was hoping that the war would come to an end. After all, the war started so that President Doe would be removed from office. However, things would not be as simple. As a matter of fact, things had become more complicated because there were now more than two groups in the fight. In fact, the fighting groups were even increasing with the addition of the ECOMOG peacekeeper force now in the mix. However, the only sign of hope was through the intervention of the ECOMOG peacekeeping force. Initially, we were strongly depending on the United States to send its military force into Liberia to stop the war. However, we would only experience disappointment because no military forces from the United States responded to Liberia to save us. Now that the ECOMOG peacekeepers were on the scene, we turned our hopes to them. We were in very desperate times, and we held on to any source of hope that we could find.

With President Doe now out of the equation, Charles Taylor now had his eyes on the presidential office. He only had to defeat the small forces that remained in the Armed Forces of Liberia (AFL), who had recently lost their leader, and the INPFL headed by Gen. Prince Johnson. Charles Taylor had control of approximately 90 percent of Liberia, and it was widely believed that he could sweep out both small forces without much effort. However, the ECOMOG peacekeepers were more determined to stop Mr. Taylor from causing bloodshed. They were more trained and had better weapons than

Charles Taylor's forces. The ECOMOG peacekeepers also joined forces with Gen. Prince Johnson to combat Charles Taylor's forces.

Eventually, things started to turn around in favor of the joint forces of ECOMOG peacekeepers and INPFL forces. The joint forces were able to eventually push Charles Taylor's forces out of Monrovia in a very short time. This was good news to hear. This meant that we would be free from Charles Taylor's regime very soon. However, it was also a very troublesome time for us at the Fendall displacement camp. Members of Charles Taylor rebel forces were very agitated, and they took their frustration out on those of us who resided on the Fendall displacement camp. They began to harass and torture those that they encountered more. There reason was because they believed that we were not supporting Charles Taylor and instead were supporting the ECOMOG peacekeepers and Gen. Prince Johnson's forces.

We all continued to listen to the evening news on BBC at 5:00 p.m. to learn what was happening. My brothers and I huddled around the small radio to listen as my father and the other adults were listening to the news. From the news, we learned that Gen. Prince Johnson's INPFL forces, with the support of the ECOMOG peacekeeping forces, were making quick advances against Charles Taylor's NPFL forces. We also learned that General Johnson forces and the ECOMOG peacekeepers were advancing toward Fendall displacement camp, where I was. This was good news to most of us at the displacement camp. This meant that we would soon be liberated from Charles Taylor's forces. I knew that General Johnson's forces were close because members of the NPFL rebels appeared to be in a high state of alertness. They were heavily armed, as if they were going to the battlefield. We were all in a state of high alertness ourselves. I often heard my father speaking to the other adults about preparing for what was to come. Whether we were going to be moving deeper into Charles Taylor's territory or get captured by General Johnson's forces. Everything was uncertain. One thing that was certain was that the battle was coming to us. We were likely going to be relocating again. I, like most of those at the Fendall displacement camp, were hoping that the displacement camp gets captured by General

Johnson's INPFL forces. That was because they were joined with the ECOMOG peacekeepers that had the support of the United States government. Most people also believed that members of the INPFL forces were less likely to commit acts of atrocities while receiving the support of ECOMOG and the international community.

We continued to live in an intense state, not knowing what would happen the next moment. Anxiety was high among most people. Our daily lives had become disrupted. There was shortage of food, water, and daily supplies. As news of the fighting came closer to our location, we decided to stay close to our room. Fewer people came into the marketplace to sell merchandise. Nongovernmental organizations such as the UN and MSF ceased coming to the camp in anticipation of the battle that was expected to come to the Fendall displacement camp. In spite of the high anticipation of the dangerous gunfight that would soon be upon us, life continued. It was only a matter of time before we had to go to the creek to take bath and do laundry. I recalled during that time that my uncle Nana took my brothers and me to the creek to take a bath. Despite the pending concerns, I had a great time playing in the water. I also noticed some teenage boys at the creek who were behaving very wild. They were jumping from the trees approximately twenty feet high and diving into the water. I thought they were different. First, I had never seen them before at the displacement camp. Secondly, they did not seem to be afraid, like most of us at the displacement camp. Most of us did not want to draw attention to ourselves, fearing that we would gain the unwanted attention of NPFL forces. We quickly came to learn that contact with NPFL rebels were often very negative. These teenagers did not seem to have those concerns. As the days went by, there appeared to be a high level of tension. The news reports kept on indicating that General Johnson forces were gaining ground and closing in on our location. During that time, we would hear small arms firing and mortar rounds in the distance. NPFL members and their supporters, who were usually family and friends, were leaving Fendall displacement camp to go further into Charles Taylor's territory. Obviously, out of concern that they would be targeted and harmed by General Johnson's force, they fled to save their lives.

One sunny and humid afternoon in November of 1990, we were sitting in our room as we would normally do. Bored with nothing to do, we sat around and had conversations. We also did not want to venture too far from our room because we could feel the tension in the air. Based on the information that we were receiving from the news, we knew that General Johnson and the ECOMOG peacekeepers would be knocking on our door very soon. The atmosphere on the displacement camp was similar to the atmosphere that we experienced before we were captured by Charles Taylor's forces. Everyone was anxious; we did not know what to expect. Everything seemed to have stopped moving. Even the air seemed still. As we were sitting anxiously in our room wondering what was to come, we started to hear small-arms firing. We all likely guessed the same, that Gen. Prince Johnson and his forces were attacking the displacement camp. When the firing persisted, we knew definitely that General Johnson forces were making a move to capture Fendall displacement camp. Fendall displacement camp was one of the largest locations with displaced Liberians, and it was a point of interest for all parties involved in the Liberian crisis. My family members and I lay low on the floor to protect ourselves from being struck by stray bullets. Although we were about to encounter a very dangerous situation, we were still hopeful that we would finally become liberated from the tyrant, who was Charles Taylor and his forces. The sound of the small arms firing became even more rapid, and I also started to hear some small explosions likely from an RPG (rocket-propelled grenade). As the gunfight intensified, I could hear the boots of soldiers running and metals clinging together. The sound of the gun firing was extremely heavy outside behind the building that my family and I were seeking shelter in. The sound was so intense that it sounded like a consistent downpour of heavy rainfall. I became curious and got up to look outside of the window that I was lying beneath. When I looked, I saw a bunch of Charles Taylor's rebel forces firing their weapons into a field. These soldiers were standing with their backs against the wall of the building that I was in. I also looked to see what they were firing at. I saw a group of soldiers, wearing green army fatigues, in a straight line like a wall approaching Charles Taylor's rebel forces. The soldiers did not seem too afraid of Charles Taylor's forces shooting at them. They did not even seek cover. They kept walking upright and firing back at Charles Taylor's forces as they approached the building. While I was looking through the window, a round struck the window that I was looking through. Uncle Nana grabbed my arm and yanked me to the floor. This was followed by a very stern look from him, as if he wanted to punish me for doing something so foolish. It was only by the grace of God that I did not get myself killed. The soldiers could have assumed that I was a member of the enemy forces and tried to shoot me. It would have been a reasonable action on the part of the soldiers. Unfortunately, me being injured or killed would have been devastating to my family.

As the fighting continued, it seemed like the battle would last forever. Finally, the sound of the explosions and heavy gun firing ceased. We were all anxious. I was very afraid, although I was hoping to get liberated from Charles Taylor's forces. I was anxious because I was not sure who had won the battle. No one came out to declare victory. So we all hunkered down on the floor in our room waiting to see which group of soldiers would show up. While we were anxiously waiting in our room, we started to hear people walking in the halls of the building. We later learned that we all had to exit the building immediately. Fear overcame me, for this was all too familiar to me. I remembered what happened a few months earlier when Charles Taylor's NPFL rebel forces took control of my neighborhood. I thought that we were all going to be liberated; instead, we were tortured. Not to forget, I also became separated from my mother, with no further information on her whereabouts. Now I seemed to be facing the same scenario again.

When we all arrived outside, the sun was very hot, and the humidity felt extremely high. We were all made to stand outside in column and wait for instructions. As we stood outside, I recognized the soldiers in their army-green fatigues, and I assumed that Gen. Prince Johnson's INPFL forces had won the battle. General Johnson forces went through the lines looking for members of Charles Taylor's forces who might have been left behind because they could not get out or were intentionally left behind to infiltrate the newly captured territory. It seemed like they knew exactly what they were looking for. As they went through the lines, they did not waste much time with my family and many of those who sought refuge at the displacement camp. General Johnson forces did locate some members of Charles Taylor's forces who were hiding among us. They were quickly taken out in a very aggressive manner. Quite often the sound of gunfire could be heard after they were taken away. I understood that to mean that they had been killed, because of my experience. While we were standing outside, it started to rain. As a young child, I started to wonder how it was possible to rain when the sun was shining brightly and it was hot. Then I heard someone in the group refer to the sudden rain as shower of blessings. I did not see who made the statement, but I believed that it must have been God that was speaking through them. Indeed, it was a blessing to be liberated from the hands of Charles Taylor and the evil individuals who represented his NPFL organization. Shortly after the rain started, a man with several bodyguards drove up in a convertible small army truck. The man got out of the truck and greeted everyone and asked how we were all doing. Then he introduced himself as Gen. Prince Johnson. He said many other things, but all that I could remember was that he was the Gen. Prince Johnson that I had heard so much about. There were so many stories about this man. I am not even sure if they were true. His stories sounded like something out of an action film like *Missing in Action*.

My experience with this new group of soldiers would be much better than the experience that I had with the previous two groups of soldiers. After we were checked and the buildings were searched, we were directed to go back into our rooms. The INPFL soldiers were very different from soldiers that I had come to encounter previously. Gen. Prince Johnson's forces were friendly and treated us like humans. It was almost as if I was living in a dream to actually experience soldiers that were nice. We were eventually able to receive food from the United Nations and other groups that donated food to us in our desperate time of need. We were in much need of food. We had not had any access to food for a long time. In fact, NPFL rebels were known to take most or all of the food that the United Nations or Medicine San Frontier (MSF) attempted to deliver to us for themselves. Therefore, many of us were very hungry and malnourished. I remember being so hungry that my ears constantly rang. My eyes felt like they were going dim. So it was certainly excellent news that food was being made available to us. My father and uncle Nana went and they were able to get some food to last us a few days. My father's friend and his nephew also went along and secured some food for their family as well. They were in a tougher situation because they had an infant daughter and another daughter who was approximately four years old. They were the most vulnerable, being the youngest among us, and it was unfortunate that they had to endure so much suffering at such a young age. As God would have it, we got news that we were going to be returning to our home in Monrovia. I was gripped with excitement when I heard this news. We all stayed on the displacement camp for a few days while the INPFL rebel forces, with the support of ECOMOG forces, cleared the camp and the surrounding area of all enemy forces. I wanted to see the peacekeepers because I was so appreciative of what they had done. I believe that many of those on the displacement camp wanted to see them and show them appreciation for intervening in the Liberian civil war and saving so many lives. We did know that the ECOMOG peacekeepers wore white helmet instead of the regular green helmet. A biblical scripture came to mind when I experienced the goodness of the ECOMOG peacekeepers. The seventh beatitudes states that "blessed are the peacemakers, for they will be called sons of God" (Matt. 5:9). Thankfully, I got the opportunity to experience what a blessing a peacemaker could be in a dire situation.

I did get to meet the ECOMOG peacekeepers as I wished. However, my first meeting with them was not as I expected. It was not as peaceful as I thought it would be. In fact, I must say that my initial encounter with them was very scary. One day, I was sitting on a desk in the classroom that my family shared with several other families. While I was sitting on the desk, I heard a loud roar over my head. I instantly jumped off the table onto the floor. For a second, I thought I was dead. I thought a mortal round had struck the building. Yet I was not injured, and the building was not damaged.

My heart was beating so fast that it felt like my heart was about to explode. I could not figure out what had just happened. The only sound that could be compare to the sound that I just heard was that of a missile shot from an artillery. I soon learned that the extremely loud noise came from a fighter jet (Alpha Jet) that was operated by ECOMOG peacekeepers fighter pilots. The jet took everyone in the room by surprise. Liberia did not own a fighter jet; therefore, I was not used to the sound of the jet. None of us were used to such strange sound. Over time, I learned that the ECOMOG fighter pilots would often turn off the engine on the jet and allow the jet to free fall. Then they would deliver a bomb and restart the jet engine as they were quickly flying away. The jet moved so fast that it seemed like it was moving at the speed of light. Luckily, the jet did not deliver any explosives; it only did a flyover. I was also able to witness the fighter jet do a few more maneuvers, including the maneuver that I experienced previously. It was actually fascinating to see in person. After it had been confirmed that the surrounding area was safe, we were informed that we could return home.

Journey Back Home

Finally, we were going to be leaving Fendall displacement camp to return home. The displacement camp was a representation of so much negative experiences for me. I couldn't wait to leave Fendall displacement camp. First of all, it never quite seemed like home. At the displacement camp, I was subjected to living with several family members and close friends in a space that was approximately the size of an average full bathroom. Also, I lived in constant fear of Charles Taylor's rebel forces daily. So it was very reasonable to understand why I would not want to be at Fendall displacement camp.

My father gathered his family together to start packing what little bit we had left. My father's friend also did the same with his family. I believe most of those on the camp were pretty excited to return home based on the many conversations among those on the camp. There was also a hint of uncertainty among all of us. We did not know if our home was still in existence or if it had been damaged by rockets. We did not have an alternate location to stay at if our home was no longer in existence. Regardless, we continued home hoping that our home was not totally damaged. There were also no jobs available. Electricity and water services were still not operational. We were still unsure if our neighborhood was really safe for us to return in spite of being assured by Gen. Prince Johnson forces that our neighborhood was safe. I still had the fear of being in my home during the middle of the night wondering if some soldiers would come to our home and harass or, even worse, cause us physical harm. However, in spite of all the uncertainties, I was still excited to return home. I had enough of the chaos at Fendall displacement camp under the leadership of

Charles Taylor. Now I was looking forward to returning home and enjoying some form of orderliness and freedom.

On the morning that we were supposed to leave Fendall displacement camp, my father, my brothers, and me went out to say goodbye to the friends that we had made. During the difficult times, we learned to depend on each other for strength, hope, and encouragement. It was sad to now separate from those that we had come to establish such close relationships with. After all, it was one of such individuals who provided the remedy that helped save the life of my father when he was ill with cholera.

After saying our goodbyes, we walked to the main road that would lead us back to our home in Monrovia. As I was walking on the main road that would lead me back to my home, I had a mixed reaction. I was excited about the idea of returning back home. However, I was also still traumatized by my initial experience on this road as I was travelling to the Fendall displacement camp. I could not get away from the trauma that I witnessed, and the visual reminder of some of my experiences was still present. However, I must admit that the road was much more cleaner than I first remembered. The shell casings were not covering the asphalts any longer. There were no longer dead bodies lying everywhere like before. A big difference was that there were no soldiers harassing and brutalizing civilians as in my previous experiences with forces connected to President Doe and Charles Taylor. I observed that members of Gen. Prince Johnson INPFL forces were very disciplined. They focused on performing their duties instead of harassing civilians. They certainly did not attempt to intimidate us, although some of them appeared intimidating to me. In all, I felt very relieved to not be harassed and tortured like I had previously experienced. I was still looking forward to seeing members of the ECOMOG peacekeeping forces. However, they were not in the front lines. They stayed in the rear and provided support since they were on a peacekeeping mission. As I anticipated meeting members of the ECOMOG peacekeeping forces, I was very grateful that during my return trip home that I did not have to worry about the challenges that I dealt with previously. Unlike the past, I was facing a whole new set of challenges that made the return trip difficult. By now, we were very malnourished, which weakened us and made the trip difficult to endure. We also lacked water and food for the long foot journey that we had embarked upon. Our trip was made even more complicated because we had an infant and a toddler with us. The infant could travel on her mother's back. However, the toddler was a little too heavy to be transported. Therefore, she had to travel on foot. It was a difficult journey to make without the adrenaline rush that we had when we were previously travelling to Fendall displacement camp. We did our best to travel as fast as we could, considering the condition of our toddler. I will always remember her as a very tough little girl for being able to endure what she had to endure. She was also a blessing to our group. She was a beautiful dark-skinned little girl with very beautiful long hair. One could barely miss her appearance because of her beauty. Soldiers were always stopping us to interact with her due to her beauty. The soldiers were offering her snacks and water. Of course, we also benefitted because we were sometimes offered water. Although we were able to get some water, it was not sufficient for the entire group. Soon, I was very thirsty again, and I felt faint. However, I understood that there was nothing that anyone could do about the thirst and hunger that I was experiencing. We were all in the same boat and needed assistance from external sources. In spite of the challenges that we were all facing, we understood that we had to toughen up so that we could make it back home. The one thing that kept me motivated was that I was able to look up and see the beautiful blue sky. The idea of being able to see the sky always gives me hope because that meant that I was still alive. Also, I was anxious to get back to the home where I had spent a large portion of my life. We walked as fast as we could to avoid being stuck outside during the night. We were still concerned about armed groups, such as Charles Taylor's NPFL members and former President Doe's soldiers harming us. We did not make it home during our trip. We settled at the home of our new friend from the Fendall displacement camp, Colonel Moore, for the night. We were fortunate that Colonel Moore resided on the outskirts of the city. I wondered what we would have done if Colonel Moore did not live in that area. It was a big relief to settle down from a full day of walking. I was thirsty and extremely hungry. Everyone was experiencing some extreme hunger. Yet we had to fetch water in large five-gallon containers from long distances. I kept drinking to fill my belly, but that strategy did not work for me at all. During those times, people did whatever they could to survive. People were cutting down the palm trees and coconut trees after eating the palm nuts and coconuts to get the soft tissue inside the tree. I am not sure how people discovered this, but it had become one of the main sources of food. The soft tissue, which was referred to as cabbage, from the palm and coconut tree was very unpleasant to me. Palm and coconut cabbage was prepared like stew. The smell and taste of the meal was one that I could not bear. At Colonel Moore's home, we were served palm cabbage stew. I was extremely hungry, so I attempted to eat the meal, but I simply could not stand the smell and taste of the stew. I simply could not eat the meal, so I ate a little bit that I could have enough strength to continue my journey the following day.

After spending the night at Colonel Moore's residence, we all woke up the following morning and got ready to complete the last phase of our journey. It was almost a perfect day, with clear blue skies. I say "almost a perfect day" because it would have been perfect had we not been experiencing such extreme hunger. Yet we continued on walking in spite of the challenges that we faced. During this part of our journey, we finally encountered the ECOMOG peacekeepers. They wore green military uniforms with white helmets. Although their white helmets were strange to me, I was still grateful that they came to help us. Many of those returning home were openly extending gratitude to the ECOMOG peacekeepers for coming to rescue us and help restore peace in Liberia.

As we continued our journey, I started to become a little excited as we got closer to our home. Our group was approaching the Congo Town community, which was the community that preceded my community. I was not very familiar with that community because my parents did not allow us to venture too far from home. However, I did recognize the German embassy and the Nigerian embassy, which was also referred to as the Nigerian House.

I also remembered that in this same area was a soldier's boot in the middle of Tubman Boulevard with the soldier's amputated leg still in the boot. It was likely a member of former President Doe's government forces. The soldier's leg had been severed. I believe that the leg was strategically placed in the middle of Tubman Boulevard to install fear in the citizens. It was such a relief to be able to walk in the streets of Monrovia without being intimidated, harassed, and tortured by hoodlums that masqueraded as freedom fighters and protectors. They were anything but what that they claimed to be.

As we approached Sophie's Ice Cream Parlor, we all started to become excited. My father reminded us that we were in our neighborhood and that we were almost home. I knew that we were almost home because I started to recognize some landmarks like Philadelphia church and the Assembly of God church. Those were the churches that I attended, so I was very aware of my surroundings. In fact, the Assembly of God church was so close to my house that I could see the church from my backyard porch. As we all walked on the asphalt road that led to my community, I became very surprised. I was actually disappointed. The grass had become overgrown. There was grass growing through the cracks on the asphalt road due to lack of usage. We also saw a few people on the way home, and we all were wondering if our neighbors would be home. We all fled without knowing of each other's destination. We also did not know if some of our relatives and friends had died due to the actions of the soldiers.

We finally made it to our home. The doors were wide open. The entire house was ransacked. We understood that this meant that members of Charles Taylor's rebels were searching our home for valuable items to loot. There were also writings on the wall inside our living room. It was very common to see writings on buildings. This was a common methods used by members of Charles Taylor's rebel forces to mark their territories. On the wall of our living room were the words "Commandos life here." We all understood that they intended to write, "Commandos live here." Sadly, the lack of decent education was a catalyst for the destructive and atrocious acts that were committed during the Liberian civil war.

Welcome Back Home

So we finally returned home. We were very excited yet very skeptical. We were skeptical because there were too many uncertainties. There was no functional government to assist us. There were no nongovernmental organizations (NGO) such as United Nations (UN) or Medicine Sans Frontier (MSN) operating in my community. There were no businesses open such as Joe Bar market, which was the major market in the area, in operation. There was also no hospital available. We still did not have access to electricity and clean drinking water. Basically, every infrastructure or organization that would have been needed to operate a society was unavailable. Of all the uncertainties that we were concern about, safety was of the most priority. Although we were relatively safe because we were now in areas under the ECOMOG peacekeepers control, we were still traumatized by the soldiers and rebels who tormented us for several months. There were rumors of government soldiers and Charles Taylor rebels robbing citizens at night or looking to cause harm to citizens. All of these circumstances gave us a real reason to be concern. How were we going to eat? Would we receive medical treatment if one of us became ill? What would we do if someone looking to cause us harm came to our home in the middle of the night? With all of these questions, the fact remains that we had no answers. There was not much that we could do to help ourselves at the time.

We did what we could do to reestablish ourselves back into our home and community. First thing was to clean up our home and prepare it for us to live in. My uncle Nana, my dad, my father's friend, and a teenage boy who was a part of my father's friend family—all worked together to clean our homes, including cutting the grass. I'm sure that it was difficult task to undertake since we were all so hungry. Back then cutting the grass was also a very difficult task. One had to swing a machete from side to side to cut the grass, which resulted in blisters developing in the palm of your hand. My father did not even have a machete or cleaning supplies. However, he improvised by using whatever he could find to clean our home before nightfall. My brothers and I also joined in and did what we could to help clean our home. During this time, we conducted an inventory of our belongings. Most of our clothing was still in our home. Surprisingly, my father's stereo set was still in his bedroom. However, many of our photos in the photo album were destroyed because of water damage.

After settling in our home, my father, my uncle, my father's friend and his nephew went out to access the neighborhood. As a leader in the community and administrative dean of the medical college, he wanted to check on the status of the medical college properties and also check on his friends in the community to see if they had return. After accessing the neighborhood, he came back to inform us that some of the buildings had been damaged, including the Seaview dormitory, which was located next to the beach. Part of the building had been destroyed by rocket explosion. My father also informed us that none of our friends in the community had return. My community resembled an abandoned town from a country Western movie. It was often referred to as a ghost town. This situation made our concerns even more real to us. With an empty community, anyone could come and do whatever they wanted to do with us, and no one would know about it. Therefore, my father made sure to find the ECOMOG peacekeepers that were stationed in our community and introduce himself to them. He later returned with some of the ECOMOG peacekeepers and introduced them to us. They were very pleasant, and their professionalism assured me that we would be safe. I am sure that my father felt the same way about the ECOMOG peacekeepers.

That evening we ate what little food that we were able to gather. Most of what we ate came from can food that we collected lying around in the abandoned homes of our community members. We were starving and dying of hunger, so we did what we had to do to survive. I was thankful that we were able to find food to eat. The food was much better than the palm cabbage that I had grown to hate. Therefore, I considered myself to have had a good day because I had the opportunity to actually eat food that was tasteful to me. After eating our meal, we later gathered around the radio to learn how the war was going. Based on the news, we learned that the General Johnson forces and the ECOMOG peacekeepers were successfully defeating Charles Taylor's forces and recapturing land from them. This news strengthened our confidence in the ECOMOG peace-keepers and made us feel protected as we settled in our abandon community. At nightfall, we lit our kerosene lantern to light up our home. It was completely black outdoors, and our house was the only home that was occupied. I didn't see any other home that appeared to be occupied on that first night.

We successfully made it through the night, and we woke up the next morning. I went out on the back porch like I used to do prior being taken captive by Charles Taylor's forces. I wanted to watch the main boulevard and see what kind of activities were going on. I believe that I really wanted to see if there were signs of life around us. I wanted to know if my household was the only occupied household in my community. However, all that I saw were military vehicles travelling on Tubman Boulevard, which was the main road that ran from the downtown area to the outskirts of the city. I was curious to know what my community looked like. I had not had a chance to go through the community. So my uncle Nana took my younger brother and me to take a tour of the disaster that had fallen on my once peaceful and beautiful neighborhood. It did not take long for me to notice the severe damage that had occurred in my community. The community was a disaster. All of the beautiful coconut trees that were along the front of my home were now cut down. The majestic palm trees that were on the side of my home were also cut down. To create a better picture of what my community looked like, I will say that it could be compare to a community that had just been struck by a hurricane. While we were exploring the neighborhood, we came across some canned-food items in a pile of trash on the road. We were extremely hungry, so we did not think twice. We started to look into the pile to see if there were any canned food that would be edible. I did not care if the cans were expired or not, if it was something that could be eaten, I was going to eat it. We opened the cans and immediately started eating. We also took some of the canned-food items home to share with our family. When we returned, my older brother told me that while we were gone, some United States Marines accompanied some journalist to our neighborhood. My older brother said that the United States marines came to our home and spoke with our father. For me that was a sign that things were going to get better. I was certain that the report by those journalists would bring attention to our conditions and our nation. We would likely get the support that we needed. At the time, we needed a lot. We needed food, water, medication; we needed clothing; and we needed protection. We needed the assistance of the United Nations and any nation or organization that would help us. We were really in a desperate situation. To find food to eat, my father and my uncle Nana would go to the swamp behind our home to catch crab and fish to cook for our daily meal. Some days they caught enough fish and crabs, and other times they did not catch enough fish and crabs. I appreciated the meals very much. I preferred the fish and crab over palm cabbage and coconut cabbage. So life was starting to look up for me. I also had the experience of having frog legs for the first time. I must say that the frog legs tasted better than I had expected. I should have known that frog legs tasted good. They were on the menu at a high-end Chinese restaurant located adjacent the St. Peter's Lutheran Church, which I attended. We never ate at that restaurant because we could not afford the restaurant. Now we were eating what was considered expensive in the poorest of conditions. What an oxymoron.

As the days went by, people started to return to their homes. I was excited because this was a sign that the community was returning to normal. However, with the return of people to the community, there was more of a need to have certain infrastructures in place. People needed food and medicine. Government facilities needed to be reopen. Schools needed to be reopen so that we could return to school. As more families returned to Monrovia, my father's friend and his family returned to their home near the airport. They felt that it was now safe enough to return to their home.

As more of the medical students, medical college employees, and neighbors returned to the community, my father started to organize them to start cleaning our community. The appearance of my community looked depressing with all the down trees, destroyed buildings, grass growing everywhere, and low population. So my father and some of the men and women started working together to clean up the neighborhood. My community consisted of the St. Joseph Catholic Hospital and the A. M. Dogliotti College of Medicine. I joined my brothers and helped in what little way that we could. Although we did not make a huge difference, we still participated in cleaning the community that we were a part of. My father was also concerned about how involved we were in the cleaning process. He was concerned about us becoming injured from mine explosions or bullets that were ignited. During cleaning, the trash would typically be burned. However, during this time, unused bullets would often ignite and discharge. Therefore, we assisted in cleaning but with a lot of caution. Unfortunately, some individuals received injuries from these stray bullets during cleaning. For this reason, my brothers and I were instructed to stay indoors during trash burning.

While my father was keeping himself busy and trying to improve the community, others were more interested in creating problems. As people became more desperate, some decided to steal from businesses and other neighbor's homes. They sometimes stole these items for themselves. They took whatever they could. They even took tiles off the wall and floor from beautiful homes that were owned by wealthy Liberians and expatriates. Every day, I saw Liberians looting from the homes of their fellow Liberians. They stole from government buildings such as the medical college and from the St. Joseph Catholic Hospital, which was immediately across the street from my home. We later learned that not all of the stolen items were for personal use. We came to learn that some members of the community had started to trade the stolen items with members of the ECOMOG forces. There were no source of income, and people started to do these things out of desperation to generate income. Many people got involve in looting because it was the only source of income. Of course, former combatants who participated in the war took advantage of the opportunity to make some money as well. They started to loot vehicles, generators, and any high-valued items that they could get their hands on. Those items were often sold to ECOMOG soldiers, who purchased the items for little or nothing.

My father did not agree with the looting that was done by his fellow Liberians, but he clearly understood the desperate need that most Liberian faced at the time. He too was also living under the same conditions. I personally could better understand stealing to provide for your family. However, stealing from your neighbor to enrich yourself was totally wrong to me. My father saw the danger in the looting that was occurring all over the city, and he decided to take a stand against it.

Dad Takes Charge

The looting by members of the community was getting out of control. It seemed like everything that could be move was getting stolen. Buildings were getting torn apart, and all the building materials were being extracted for personal use or sold to ECOMOG peacekeepers. Some of the looted properties were also sold to the few Liberians who could afford to buy these stolen valuables for next to nothing. The high level of greed or desperate behavior was resulting in further destruction of community. I often heard my father speak about his frustration to some of the people in the neighborhood. He was concerned that the already-challenged Liberian government would be unable to replace the items that were stolen from various facilities. Some of those items were essential to the operation of those facilities. My father predicated that a previously struggling government would be even more challenged as a result of the recent civil war. This would definitely make it very difficult for a government under such condition to be capable of successfully functioning. My father eventually had enough of the looting and decided to do something about it. "Take no part in the unfruitful works of darkness, but instead expose them" (Eph. 5:11 ESV). My father decided to put his frustration into action. He recruited the few men in the community to form a neighborhood watch team. Initially, he was not very successful. First of all, there were not many people in the community. The few men who had returned were busy taking care of their families or participating in the looting. Others were too afraid to get involve because some of those looting were former combatants. So my father settled with starting a neighborhood watch team with

86

himself and Uncle Nana. It was pretty risky since it was only the both of them, considering that some of those who they would encounter were former soldiers who were known murderers. The fear was that some of these looters still had access to weapons. I feared that if my father aggravated these soldiers, they would return at night to harm us. However, my stubborn father was not deterred by the risk of violence against him. He continued to put himself in harm's way by confronting looters who came to loot at both the St. Joseph Catholic Hospital and the A. M. Dogliotti Medical School. Well, my father did receive treats from looters. It even got to the point where my brothers and I started to receive some of those threats from some of those looters. Some of those looters were even members of the community and knew my family well. These looters did not appreciate my father preventing them from making money, and they were not going to sit and allow my father to stop them without a fight. I believe that my brothers and I received threats because we were easier targets. They certainly did not want to deal with my father who was well-known to be a no-nonsense kind of person. I personally was not afraid because I trusted that my father would protect us if anyone attempted to harm us.

Eventually, my father was able to influence some to the returning neighbors to join him on the neighborhood watch team. One hot afternoon, my father learned that some individuals were attempting to steal two large generators from the St. Joseph Catholic Hospital. He quickly responded to the hospital to stop the men from stealing the generators. Fortunately, the generators were very large, and the men were having a difficult time loading both generators into their pickup truck. My father was able to successfully prevent the men from stealing the generators. However, this time the encounter was different. The men stated that my father was behaving as if his father owned the hospital. They also threatened that they would return to take care of my father later. My father stated that they were not afraid to be looting and that their demeanor led him to believe that the men were former soldiers. My father took the threat seriously, and he went to the ECOMOG peacekeeper station. He met with the commanding officer at the station and informed them about the incident and the threats made by the looters. The commanding officer dispatched some soldiers to be assigned to our immediate neighborhood. My father also provided housing for the soldiers in the A. M. Dogliotti Medical College Seaview dormitory, which was located right on the beach. The dormitory was called Seaview dormitory because it was right on the shores of the Atlantic Ocean. It was also a strategic location because looters, and even soldiers, used the beaches at night to gain entry or escape when committing crime. The decision to have the ECOMOG peacekeepers embedded in my neighborhood was essential. It automatically stopped the rampant looting that was occurring in my community, and it also calmed the fear of members of the community that were concerned about been harassed by former combatants. It also eased the treats that were being made against my father and our family.

My father went even further. He recruited members of the ECOMOG peacekeepers and went throughout the community to the homes of those individuals who were involved in looting and recovered items that were stolen from the St. Joseph Catholic Hospital and the A. M. Dogliotti Medical College campus. My father did this because he understood that those institutions would need all the assistance that they could get if they were going to reopen. To reduce the opportunity for looters to infiltrate the community during the night and commit crime, a curfew was put in place. With the security measures that were put in place by the ECOMOG peacekeeper, my father and many of the members of the community felt safer. In fact, my father believed that those security measures would create a suitable environment for the hospital and the medical college to reopen sooner than later. This was just a wishful thought, of course. Everyone had fled the area, and my father did not know if or when those institutions would reopen. All we knew was that the hospital staff had fled the country. It was very possible that the hospital would not reopen since the hospital was operated by foreign staff. However, my father, in his wisdom, believed that it would be better to have those institutions in the best conditions that they could be in.

As the weeks went by, more people continued to return to Monrovia. This was the result of Gen. Prince Johnson's INPFL forces and the ECOMOG peacekeepers capturing more territories from Charles Taylor's NPFL forces. As more people returned to the community, the United Nations also returned to the community to assess conditions. I'm sure they quickly realized how drastic our conditions were. In a few days after the United Nation's visit, we received good news that we would soon be receiving much needed food supplies. My father volunteered to work along with members of the United Nations. He provided storage locations at the medical college campus for the supplies to be stored for distribution. It was also the most suitable location available at the time because the ECOMOG peacekeepers, who resided on the medical college campus, provided free security.

By the grace of God, our prayers were finally answered. The food and medical supplies that we had needed for so long had finally arrived. On the day that the supplies were distributed, there was a feeling of happiness among the people in the community. Most of the older teenagers and young adults in my community went to the distribution center to get food and medical supplies for their love ones. My father was also able to obtain some rice and other food supplies for our family. Since our return back to our home, we had been surviving on minimal food supplies. Now we had the first opportunity to have some decent food available to us. After the food was distributed, my father and uncle Nana returned home with food such as white rice, chicken, powder milk, cornmeal, and cans of sardines. Of course, the rice was the most important food since it is the staple food in Liberia. In fact, rice is commonly referred to as gold dust because of its value in Liberia.

We were all so happy that we had received food that we celebrated by preparing a big meal. My father and my uncle Nana cooked rice with stew, and we ate as if we had never eaten before. This was the first time that we had a decent meal since we were captured by Charles Taylor's NPFL forces in early august of 1990. I went back for seconds and thirds; I just could not get enough. I was not the only one indulging in this feast. Everyone in my home was also partaking in the indulgence. The following day after the feast, I experienced an upset stomach early in the morning. I felt horrible. It was the price that I paid for overindulging. Other members of my family also experienced upset stomach as a result of overeating. It was a busy day for the single bathroom in our home. After we recovered from our days of indulgence, we went back to being more moderate with our meal. After all, we had to manage our meal so that it could last for a longer period. Although we had food currently, food was still scares. We were all conscious of this, and we did not want any food to be wasted.

Conditions continued to improve. More Liberians kept returning to Monrovia. The ECOMOG peacekeepers were now in total control of security in Monrovia. Members of Gen. Prince Johnson's INPFL forces and former president Doe's loyal government forces, AFL (Armed Forces of Liberia), were now disarmed and removed from active service. With our local Liberian armed men and women out of the streets, I felt more confident that the ECOMOG forces were in total control of Monrovia. An interim government was also put in place to govern the nation, although they were really only governing areas under the control of ECOMOG peacekeepers. The reality was that Charles Taylor had control of a large portion of Liberia. This resulted in Liberia becoming separated. Those in Charles Taylor's held territories were not allowed to cross over into ECOMOG-held territories. However, those in Monrovia had the freedom to go into Charles Taylor's territories. Although it was consider a very dangerous decision, some did it for desperate reasons. Sometimes people were detained and even harmed by Charles Taylor's forces for crossing the borderline that separated the two territories. For this reason, many families were separated although they were in the same country. Out of desperation, people still attempted to cross over into Monrovia to become reunited with their love ones. Those who were successfully able to escape from Charles Taylor's territory were considered to be liberated because they were able to escape from been held captive by Charles Taylor's forces. This situation also affected my family in many ways. There were many relatives that we were unable to reconnect with, such as my paternal grandmother who was living by herself in the Totota area. Of course, the ability of my father to continue searching for my mother was greatly hindered because of the division within Liberia. My father was unable to go behind Charles Taylor's territory because he had to take care of us. He was the only parent that we had, and we were all very young. Another challenge would have been finding someone to provide care for three children during a time when most were unable to provide for their own families. It was very unfortunate; however, this was the situation in which we found ourselves.

As the year 1990 came to an end, life started to quickly improve. Thanks to the ECOMOG peacekeepers, more people felt secure enough to return to Monrovia. The interim government headed by Dr. Amos Sawyer was receiving a lot of support from the international community, who were to assist with the redevelopment of Monrovia. There were often reports on the news of some government offices reopening. Several nongovernmental organizations were hinting of coming to Monrovia to provide services to the people of Liberia who desperately needed assistance. During that time, I learned that Dr. Amos Sawyer was coming to visit the community. My father, who was one of the leaders of the community, informed my brothers and me that the interim president, Dr. Amos Sawyer, was coming to assess conditions on the ground. It was pretty exciting for me. After my brothers and I learned about Dr. Sawyer's visit, it was all that we could talk about. My brothers and I were careful not to tell people about the interim president's future visit. We clearly understood that my father only knew this information because he was one of the community leaders and that it was not meant to be known by everyone. It was one of the benefits of having a father who was a community leader. We had the opportunity to learn very important information early, which was often a plus in an environment filled with uncertainties.

The following day I woke up filled with excitement. I stayed close to home so that I could have an opportunity to see the presidential convoy arrive, as my home was located at the entrance of the community. I also had a pretty good view of the front of the St. Joseph Catholic Hospital, where the interim president was likely going to be speaking with members of the community. Later during the day, Dr. Amos Sawyer arrived at the hospital. It was exciting to see the fancy

91

cars in the presidential convoy. As a child, I always admired members of the presidential security team. I thought that they looked cool. It appeared that my recent encounter with dangerous soldiers from the government force and Charles Taylor's force did not change my view of all soldiers. Obviously, soldiers rescued me; therefore, I knew that not all soldiers were evil. Upon arrival, interim president Dr. Amos Sawyer met with some of the members of the community. I was able to see the interim president from my back porch as he took a tour of the hospital. After the visit, the interim president left the community, and our day of excitement concluded. When my father returned home, my brothers and I were very excited that our father had spoken with the interim president. We asked him about the meeting, and he told us that the interim president reassured him that things were going to start improving. Dr. Amos Sawyer was certainly right.

Shortly after the interim president's visit, the brothers who managed the St. Joseph Catholic Hospital returned to assess the hospital property. When my father saw that they had returned, he was excited that they had returned. He went to see them. He had known them for many years. This visit brought hope to my father that the hospital might reopen. The reopening of the hospital was very important because at the time there were no hospitals in Monrovia. Brother Jose Sebastian, who ran the hospital, was a part of the team that came to assess the hospital property. After conducting the assessment, Brother Jose informed my father that he had a positive review after the assessment. According to my father, Brother Jose informed him that because the roof, buildings, and major equipment such as the generators were still intact, it was likely that the staff would return and reopen the hospital. However, he had to return to Spain and provide a report to his superiors before a final determination could be made. I was happy that my father took the bold step to protect the hospital property. I believe that had he not protected the hospital properties, the roof, floor, wall tiles, and steel rods would have been ripped out. This would have definitely discouraged the hospital staff from returning. Most members of the community hoped that the hospital would reopen because it was a better hospital than the John F. Kennedy (JFK) Hospital. JFK Hospital was a government-ran hospital, and government institutions were known to be poorly ran. JFK Hospital was not known to be dependable, and the citizens wanted a hospital that they could depend on. Also, the government of Liberia was still not fully functional, and no one knew when JFK Hospital would reopen. I was really excited about the idea of the St. Joseph Catholic Hospital reopening. For me, the reopening of the hospital brought back a sign of normalcy to the community.

After a few weeks, Brother Jose and a team from the hospital returned to hospital property. This time Brother Jose came to our home and chatted with my brothers and me. Then he left with my father, and they both went to join the others at the hospital. After their meeting, my father returned home looking very excited. He always had a big smile on his face when he was excited. I anticipated that he would inform us that the hospital would reopen. When my father spoke to my brothers and me, he confirmed my thoughts that the hospital would be reopening. Not only did he confirm my thoughts, he also informed us that Brother Jose hired him to be the property manager for the hospital properties. This was very good news since the government was not operating. Now God had blessed my father with the opportunity to provide for his family. A job with the hospital was even more beneficial than a government job at the medical college because the hospital had better pay and benefits while the government was unreliable in compensating its employees. With no jobs available, my father now had a very reliable job with excellent benefits. "And my God will supply every need of yours according to his riches in glory in Christ Jesus" (Phil. 4:19 ESV). I actually preferred that my father be employed by the hospital; however, the position provided to him was only temporary. While the position that he was offered was well below his qualification, he gladly accepted it so that he could be able to provide for his family and help the community by protecting the hospital property. My father also told us that Brother Jose verified that the hospital reopening largely depended on the fact that the two large generators at the hospital were still there. According to Brother Jose, the hospital would not have reopened as quickly as it did if the generators were stolen because they were very expensive. After hearing this, I appreciated the wisdom of my father even more. So my father took care of the hospital property and protected the property from looters that were out to earn some extra income. Times were hard, but looting properties was not helpful to the restoration of Monrovia. My father was also allowed to hire a few men to clean and protect the property. So my father hired a few men including my uncle Nana to take care of the hospital property.

Now that my father had a source of income, my family's living conditions improved. We could now afford regular meals. This was no small thing. Most people in Monrovia did not have this luxury. I watched how dedicated my father was to his new position. He showed no pride. Instead, he showed his gratefulness through his dedication. "Whatever your hand finds to do, do it with your might" (Eccles. 9:10 ESV). I saw my father wake up daily and go to the hospital, cleaning and managing the men he had hired to help him get the hospital property in order. I also saw my father getting closer to God during this time. My father had made a vow to God that he would give up drinking alcoholic beverages if God protected him and rescued our family from Charles Taylor and his soldiers. After we were rescued from Charles Taylor forces, my father kept his promise to God. My father had to grow closer to God, not only because our family needed protection and provision. I believe that my father felt that he needed strength and guidance from God to enable him to make it through the sudden and difficult challenges that life had brought him. My father was having a very difficult time dealing with the forced separation and uncertainty of my mother's whereabouts. It was too tough of a burden for him to bear. Without the strength of God, I do not believe that my father would have made it. My father and mother were very close. They had been together since high school. Now he was left to be without the woman that he was supposed to have spent the rest of his life with. In spite of all the challenges that he was enduring, I saw my father portray strength and continue to do whatever he could to take care of his family. My father continued to work as the property manager until the hospital was ready to be reopened. It was a great advancement for the city to finally have an established medical facility such as the St. Joseph Catholic Hospital operating.

As the hospital was reopening, other institutions such as churches and schools started to work toward reopening as well. Initially, one school opened to rehabilitate students because they had been exposed to so many atrocities. My father thought that we needed this rehabilitation; therefore, he sent us to the school. Many of the kids in my community had returned, and they also attended the school. The school also allowed me the opportunity to refresh and prepare me for getting back into school. In my community, all the kids attended the Assembly of God Mission (AGM) School. The school was only walking distance and located in my community. I was excited to return to school. It was actually fun to return to school and meet new friends. Returning to school provided me the opportunity to focus on something else besides the negative impact of the civil war. I was ready to return to school so that I continue to work hard and prove myself. I still had the mindset that I wanted to overcome my failure and do extremely well in my grades. In the end, my hard work paid off. I finished the program as one of the top student in the class.

The environment started to become more normal. The interim government also started to become more operational, opening a few government offices in Monrovia. The medical college had not reopened. It was not a top priority at the time. However, there was some planning going on. At least, it gave my father hope that the institution was reopening. Thankfully, he had employment at the Catholic hospital, which was a great help to our family. I will admit that life in Monrovia was not what it used to be. However, we were able to find things to do to keep us entertained. I started becoming interested in basketball. I develop love for the game by watching my uncle Nana playing prior to the civil war. I also became introduced to the NBA and the cool basketball shoes that I saw in the sport magazines. My brothers and I started playing basketball with the son of a Canadian doctor who had just moved in the neighborhood. He was much bigger than we were but that did not stop me from challenging him on the court. There were also many recreational centers established by nongovernmental organizations (NGO) to help rehabilitate youths in Monrovia. The most popular recreational center was located at the American Corporation School (ACS) located across the street from Cabral Estate in Monrovia. Many of the youths in the city were not privileged enough to have access to such institution. I was one of such youth. Therefore, I went to ACS to enjoy and have fun at the location. However, I also went to check out the property because I was never able to see what was on the other side of the fence. It was a beautiful school campus, and it was everything that I imagined it to be. The school also had a large indoor basketball court with hardwood flooring. It was the first time I had seen one, and I enjoyed playing on it. My brothers and I used to go there every Sunday to hang out and play basketball. There was also loud music playing on speakers and movies as well. This was one of my best experiences in postwar Liberia. The other recreational locations were the beautiful beaches in Monrovia. However, my brothers and I were not allowed to go there due to fear of us drowning. I understood my father's reason for making this rule because too many children had drowned in the Atlantic Ocean. I saw so many kids crying because they had lost a friend in the ocean. I once lost a close friend and classmate in the Atlantic Ocean. It was very sad for my classmates and me because we used to have lots of fun times together.

Eventually, the Atlantic Ocean took someone even more close to me. One Sunday afternoon, my uncle Nana told my father that he was taking my brothers and me to visit my cousin in Cabral Estate, which was across the street from the American Corporation School (ACS). On our way to my cousin's house, my uncle Nana told my brothers and me that he was going to hang out at the beach. Uncle Nana also instructed us to go to our cousin's house and wait for him to pick us up. So we did as we were instructed. As the day came to an end, it started to get dark. Uncle Nana had not returned, so we decided to leave for home. When we returned home, I noticed that something was wrong. Everyone seemed very serious. One of the neighbors asked us about Uncle Nana, and we told him that we did not know where he was. We informed him that Uncle Nana told us that he was going to the beach. My father later returned and gave us the sad news that Uncle Nana had drowned in the Atlantic Ocean. I later learned that my uncle died while trying to save other swimmers from drowning. My uncle was invincible to me. He was a tough guy, and I learned everything from him. He was a musician, bodybuilder, basketballer, martial arts black-belt holder, and a strong swimmer. So it was unbelievable to me that he would drown. His death really pained me. He was the only one who I could talk to when I was feeling sad. He was my greatest cheerleader. Uncle Nana taught me to never give up and to always keep on trying.

Of course, some attributed his death to witchcraft. He was discovered the following day on the shores of the Atlantic Ocean with large chunks of his body missing. This discovery provided support to those who believed that his death was caused by witchcraft. In Liberia, everything negative seems to occur because of the practice of witchcraft. I personally believe that his drowning was a result of a shark attack. He was a strong swimmer and physically strong. Therefore, it was more reasonable for me to believe that he was attacked by sharks. It was a very sad time for my family. Once again, we had lost another member of our family. The second in two years. This also had a heavy impact on my father. My uncle was like a son to him. Not only had my father lost a son, he had also lost a helper. With my mother taken away from our family, my uncle stepped in and assisted my father in providing care for us. Now my uncle was no longer with us, and my father had to do it all alone.

Life changed for all of us. My brothers and I had to take up more responsibilities. I had to get water for our home. I had to roll a sixty-liter drum that weighed a lot more than me. However, water was a necessity, and I had to do what had to be done to supply my home with water. My siblings and I shared the responsibility of supplying our home with water. I believe that those chores taught us to become determined and learn responsibility.

Hope for Mom

Life in Monrovia continued to improve. More Liberians were escaping from Charles Taylor's territory into the ECOMOG peacekeepers territory. Although the fighting had stopped, life under Charles Taylor's control was still dangerous. Families were separated and approximately 70 percent of those in Liberia were under Charles Taylor's control. Of course, there was always the fear that Charles Taylor might one day attempt to take control of Monrovia. After all, it was the only thing stopping him from gaining total control of the nation. For now, things were moving in a positive direction in Liberia. Government offices were reopening in Monrovia. My father also started to prepare for the reopening of the medical college while still working at the St. Joseph Catholic Hospital. By now, the hospital was fully operating. Although many of the previous doctors who were expatriates did not return, there were many new doctors and their families who moved into the community. That was good for my siblings and me because most of the doctors had children my age.

The medical school eventually reopened, and my father resumed his duties as the administrative dean of students affairs. Also, at the hospital, there was an availability for an administrator. The previous personnel director did not return to Monrovia after the initial civil war. Like many others who had the opportunity to leave Liberia, he fled when he had the chance. Brother Jose offered the position to my father. The position was great because it paid much more than the medical college. The position also came with a fully furnished home that included electricity and running water. This was a big plus as majority of the homes in Liberia did not have such amenities. This would have brought life close to what it used to be. My sibling and I were so excited at this new opportunity. However, my father had a different idea. He put the needs of the people above his own by choosing to forsake the new house and all of the amenities that it offered so that the hospital could provide housing for an additional doctor. The hospital typically provided housing for the doctors because they were often on call and needed to respond quickly. Obviously, my father made the decision for a worthy cause. However, I was being selfish, and I disapproved of my father's decision. I wanted to make my life easy and relieve myself of the burdens of carrying large barrels of water for long distances and using kerosene lantern to read. However, my father was not one to keep us away from hard work. After all, my grandmother did not keep him away from hard work, and now he was passing down the custom to us. He certainly learned the benefit of hard work, and I'm sure that he did not want us to miss out on those benefits.

After my father acquired the new position at the hospital, he was able to afford better education for my brothers and me. The school that I attended prior to the civil war was about to reopen. Therefore, I began the process of returning to Calvary Baptist Church School. However, that plan was disrupted by an encounter with someone that would cause a major influence in my life.

One day after doing my daily chores, I was walking in front of my home hanging out in my neighborhood. The front of my home was a common path that was used by all to travel through the community. While I was walking in front of my house, I came across Sister Shirley Kolmer. She was also walking in front of my home toward the beach to visit the S. M. A. Father's residence. I was surprised when she slowed down and started to walk along the side of me. I had no choice but to notice her. She had quite a presence; she was a very tall female. I was surprised because, although we were somewhat familiar, she had never initiated a conversation with me before. She asked me about school and how I was doing in school. It seemed like she wanted to know more about my education. She asked me what school I went to, what grade I was in, and how my grades were. I responded to her barrage of questions without really

thinking much of them. This was pretty typical for a child growing up at the time. Fortunately for me, I was now in the position
to provide a favorable response when it came to my grades. During
our conversation, she suggested that I take the entrance exam to St.
Patrick's High School since I was going into the seventh grade. She
also informed me that she had been watching me and that she had
observed my hard work and discipline as I did my chores. Her words
were very encouraging to me, especially because I knew that she was
the principal of St. Patrick's High School. I also reasoned that since
she would know what it took to be a student at St. Patrick's High
School, I would have a good chance at making it in St. Patrick's High
School. I had always admired St. Patrick's High School, but I never
really thought about attending the school. The thought of attempting to attend St. Patrick's High School was very intimidating to me.
Those who attended St. Patrick's High School were usually the best
of the best. St. Patrick's High School would often win any academic
competition because they had such academically gifted students. In
spite of the fear that I had regarding attending St. Patrick's High
School, I felt encouraged after my conversation with Sister Shirley
Kolmer.

After my conversation with Sister Shirley Kolmer, I started to
encourage my younger brother to take the St. Patrick's entrance exam.
Then my younger brother and I spoke to my father about taking the
exam. He appeared very impressed, and he agreed to us taking the
entrance exam. He always supported us, especially when it came to
our education. We took the exam, but we also applied to return to
Calvary Baptist Church School as a backup plan. By the grace of
God, we both passed the entrance exam and were able to get into St.
Patrick's High School. The experience of applying to and getting into
St. Patrick's High School taught me a very valuable lesson. I learned
not to be held back by fear and discomfort. I learned that I could do
anything that I set my mind to. What's the worst that could happen?
If I did not pass the exam, I could always try again. The next time I
would have a better chance of passing the test because I would now
have experience. The institution also left a lasting impression in my
life, one that continued to influence me until this day.

Life was getting better in the capital city of Monrovia in spite of lacking some essential services such as electricity and running water. I, like most people in the city, did the best that could be done to make myself comfortable. My father was working at both St. Joseph Catholic Hospital and the medical college. He was a busy man, but he was always available to us. He also never forgot about my mother. One day, he told my brothers and me that he had a dream that my mother was in a place in Ivory Coast called Danane. My father was unfamiliar with the name; therefore, he asked around to see if this was a real place. He was later able to confirm that Danane was a real place in the nation of Ivory Coast. I was very excited. For me, this was a revelation from God, and I had a strong belief that God was revealing the whereabouts of my mother. The challenge was getting to Danane to find my mother. At the time, there were no commercial flights getting out of Liberia. Also, even if there were flights available, my father did not have the funds to fly to Ivory Coast and spend several days or weeks to search for her. He was all that we had. I wondered who would have provided for us while he was gone. The only other option to get to the Ivory Coast would have been to travel by road through Charles Taylor's territory. However, this would not have been the best choice considering the previous experiences that we had with the soldiers. Therefore, my father did the only thing that he could do. He spoke to his employers at the St. Joseph Catholic, and he explained his story to them about his wife. My father asked the brothers at the hospital if they could assist him in going to Danane and searching for his wife. At the time, Danane was a location in Ivory Coast where many displaced Liberians settled in as refugees from the war in Liberia. The Catholic organization was also operating in Danane, providing assistance to Liberian refugees. The brothers from the St. Joseph Catholic Hospital were only able to agree to assist my father by searching for my mother while serving in Danane. That evening my father returned home and told my brothers and me that members from the Catholic mission agreed to assist us in looking for mother in Danane. It was a great opportunity for us because the Catholic organization had access to planes, and they could quickly fly from Liberia to Ivory Coast without needing a commercial airline. I had very high hopes that my mother would be found. My father frequently had dreams that would come to pass, and I strongly believed that this dream would be no different. After all, how coincidental was it that my father would dream that my mother was in a place that actually existed but he had no prior knowledge of? I saw this revelation as an answered prayer.

A few days before members of the Catholic organization flew to Ivory Coast, my father gathered a few photos that clearly showed my mother's face and gave it to them. My brothers and I assisted my father in selecting the photos. I was very anxious but hopeful during this time. Now all that I could do was wait for the Catholic staff to return, hopefully, with my mother. The Catholic staff would be leaving for a few months. I experienced a high level of anxiety during those months. I was wondering what my initial reaction would be when I finally saw my mother after so many months of being separated. I thought about the stories that my father, brothers, and I would exchange with my mother. I imagined that we would have so much to say to each other that we could be talking for days. The anticipation was killing me. However, I had no choice but to wait with high hopes for the return of my mother. During this period, I continued to ask my father if he had received any news to confirm that my mother had being located. I am sure that my father was anxious as well, but he had to continue to depict stability in his emotions and be strong for us.

A few weeks later, the Catholic staff returned from Danane, Ivory Coast. My father met with them, and he learned that they were unsuccessful in their attempt to locate her. That evening my father had the unfortunate task of informing us that our mother was not located. I am sure that he was disappointed and did not want to provide such disappointing news to his children. This was a very difficult thing to do, but it certainly had to be done. After my father revealed that my mother was not located, I felt very disappointed. However, I did not lose hope that she was in Danane, Ivory Coast. I still believed that the revelation about mother being in Danane, Ivory Coast, was from God. I believe that a revelation from God could not be untrue. So I continued to believe that my mother was alive, and that she was at some point in Danane, Ivory Coast. I understood that the Catholic missionaries searched for my mother but could not locate her. That did not mean that she was not in Danane, Ivory Coast. It simply meant that they did not find her.

Operation Octopus

Although the news that Mom was not located was devastating, I continued to move forward with life. We all did; we had to. Life in the city was getting back on track as best as it could. We missed a few essentials such as running water and supply of electricity that had not yet been restored. However, most of the city was fully operating. Most government offices had opened. Most schools had also reopened. Many businesses had also reopened. I still missed my favorite business, Sophie's Ice Cream, which had not reopened. Many of the embassies in my neighborhood also did not reopen. I surely missed having new friends although they often change. However, I still had my old neighborhood friends to play with. I also made some new friends who were children of the hospital staff that were new to hospital. These new friends quickly replaced the old ones, and we would come to establish relationships that would last a lifetime. I also came to establish very close relationships with many of my classmates from St. Patrick's High School and my previous school, Calvary Baptist Church School. Many of those friends I am still currently in touch with.

I had just become a teenager, and I was just starting to enjoy my independence. My father allowed my brothers and me the freedom to venture a lot further from home by ourselves than I believe my mother was willing to allow. I started playing basketball and gaining much interest in it. I quickly started playing at various basketball courts around Monrovia and making new friends. I also joined the community basketball team, playing with some older teenagers and young adults. I remember having so much fun during this time of my life in spite of the civil war. Because of my interest in basketball, I also joined my class team at St. Patrick's High School. It was very unusual for most of the teenage boys in Liberia to be interested in basketball. Soccer was the dominant sports; therefore, most of the kids played soccer. As for me, my connection to basketball was very strong. Sometimes, I believe that it was a way to connect with my late uncle Nana, who was very influential in the early stages of my life.

On October 14, 1992, I was preparing to play my first organized basketball game in my school, intramural basketball tournament. I had spent that day preparing for my game. My class was going to play against my brother's class. Of course, we had spent all day trash talking one another and arguing about which class team would win the game. My younger brother and I even played a little bit of basketball that evening to sharpen our skills for the basketball game the following day. On October 15, 1992, I woke up early in the morning to clean my basketball sneakers for the game. It was a common practice in Liberia to take very good care of your shoes and clothing. Many Liberians did not have the money to afford multiple shoes and clothing, so most Liberians took excellent care of their possessions. In addition, Liberian culture dictates that you maintain excellent appearance. So many Liberians put a lot of attention and effort on their outward appearance. This is a very good thing, but when done excessively, it could be a bad thing. Unfortunately, I have observed that the focus of my fellow Liberians on outward appearance have hindered us from developing those inward characteristics that are so essential to our personal growth.

As I was cleaning my sneakers at approximately 6:00 a.m., I heard an explosion in the direction of the Congo Town community. The Congo Town community was just east of my neighborhood. I initially paused to figure out what was going on. I was very sure that the sound was an explosion from a mortar round. My heart sunk. I began to question myself. Was I about to experience the horrifying circumstances that I endured during the 1990 war? I did not know what was going on. Although I was certain that what I heard was an explosion from a mortar round, I kept hoping that it was just a mistake. Shortly after the explosion, some of the neighbors came out and stated that they too had heard the explosion, confirming my fear. I became anxious and started to become fearful that things were going back to the devastation that I experienced as I walked to the Fendall displacement camp. My father also got up and went to the hospital to see what news he could learn. My father quickly returned home and informed us that Charles Taylor's forces had attacked Monrovia. I immediately understood that my brothers and I would not be going to school. In fact no one would be going to school. School was everyone's least concern. However, I was still somewhat disappointed that I did not get to play my first official basketball game. Nevertheless, I had other matters that were more concerning than playing a game.

Later that day, I gathered around the radio with some of my neighbors, and we all listed to learn what was going on. After listening to the news, I learned that Charles Taylor had waged war against the ECOMOG peacekeepers. They were the only force that was preventing him from accomplishing his main goal, which was to take over Liberia and became the president. Once the ECOMOG peacekeepers were driven out of Monrovia, Liberia would be under his control. Charles Taylor was not going to allow any foreigner to keep him from becoming president of Liberia. He was willing to do whatever it took to get what he wanted. I recall that during an interview on the radio, Charles Taylor stated that he was going to take over Monrovia and flush the Liberians in Monrovia and the ECOMOG peacekeepers into the Atlantic Ocean. Fear gripped me when I heard this statement. Because of my experience, I did not take it lightly that Charles Taylor was capable of doing what he stated during his interview. I had come to learn that Charles Taylor was wicked enough to do what he stated. The loss of life would not mean anything to him. Most of us living in Monrovia feared greatly for our lives. We had all right to be fearful because many of us had recently experienced the atrocities of the 1990 civil war. The savages who called themselves Freedom Fighters were all but what they claimed to be. They were brutal and full with rage and greed. The thought of these savages returning to take control of Monrovia was scary. During this time, I experienced a very high level of anxiety because the threat posed by Charles Taylor and his force was a very real possibility.

The thought of Charles Taylor taking over Monrovia was not all that I had to be concerned about on October 15, 1992. I also had to deal with the reality of the situation that I was presented with on that day. The strategy used by Charles Taylor to attack Monrovia could only be described as evil genius. Charles Taylor force was the largest in Liberia. He had more soldiers than any other group involved in the Liberian civil war, and he knew that the morale among his men was very high. He was very popular among his supporters, even until this day. He also knew that he had the resources to provide ammunition for his soldiers. Charles Taylor had commanded his forces to surround the city of Monrovia, leaving only the Atlantic Ocean accessible. I believe that the only reason why he did not attack Monrovia from the Atlantic Ocean was because he did not have a naval force. I was even more grateful that Charles Taylor did not have an air force. Charles Taylor and members of his organization possessing such capability would have likely resulted in atrocities beyond anyone's imagination. Therefore, Monrovia was attacked by all possible ground locations. With residents having nowhere to run, Charles Taylor and his NPFL forces launched several long-range missiles into Monrovia. The missiles were launched indiscriminately throughout Monrovia at all times of the day. My family and I tried to find shelter, but there were not too many places in Monrovia that one could hide from such a weapon. The missiles exploded upon impact and resulted in maximum damage. A building with a basement would have been a preferable location to take shelter, but such buildings were not very common in Liberia. This created a completely new set of challenge. We were unable to seek shelter in my home or in a building like in the past. We had to quickly adapt to our new situation.

We were all confused because we had never experienced anything like this before. Instead of running from foot soldiers shooting automatic assault rifles, we were now running from soldiers firing missiles from far away. Typically, one did not experience the impact of the battle if the battle was not going on in your neighborhood. Now it did not matter where you were, you experienced the impact just the same. Charles Taylor and his close generals and associates thought it wise to employ this evil strategy in spite of the potential to cause large-scale destruction to lives and properties. The attack was nicknamed Operation Octopus because the city of Monrovia was attacked from all sides, excluding the Atlantic Ocean, like an octopus tentacles.

On the first day of the Operation Octopus, we repeatedly heard sounds of missiles whistling in the air. Those whistling sounds were usually followed by very loud explosions. Each time I heard the whistling from the missiles, my heart sunk. That was because I knew what was next. Unfortunately, you never knew where the rocket was going to land. I can't remember how many missiles fell around us on that day, but they were many. Typically, during a battle, one might experience a missile falling in their neighborhood once or twice. However, this time it was like missile launching on steroids. All day long, cars, ambulances, and military vehicles were speeding to the St. Joseph Catholic Hospital carrying wounded individuals. Individuals were also seen carrying their love ones in wheelbarrows to the hospital for treatment because of injury from Charles Taylor's missiles attack. So many men, women, and children were brought to the hospital throughout the day. I even saw one of my childhood friends who was wounded from the missile attack. He had a cut behind one of his ears and other parts of his body. He had been struck by a shrapnel from the missile explosion, which sliced him behind one of his ears. He was lucky to be alive. I could only wonder how traumatic it must be for him to continue to hear the sound of missiles whistling in the air. My friend experience also quickly reminded me of the very real possibility that I too could become injured like my friend or even killed. With missiles raining down on us, this was very possible.

During this time, I turned to God for his divine protection in my life. I joined many in Monrovia to pray in my home and in church for God to protect us from Charles Taylor and his invasion. I, along with many of those who resided in Monrovia during that time, undoubtedly understood that a victory for Charles Taylor and his NPFL forces would be disastrous for Monrovia and its people. On the first night of Operation Octopus, the attack intensified. Although the missiles had ceased for a period during the evening, it resumed after midnight. I remembered that night. I was very tired, but I was afraid to go to sleep. I was afraid because I believed that the missiles would start falling again. After all, they had been falling all day long. I did not want to go to sleep and get caught off guard. However, the fatigue overpowered me, and I eventually fell asleep. That night I remembered my father waking up my brothers and me in the middle of the night. My father told us to hurry and run outside of our home. Although I did not know why he was asking us to run outside, I could only assume that it was because of a missile attack. After all, we were under Charles Taylor's missile attack. That night fear gripped me. My current situation looked all too familiar. This situation reminded me about when my family was captured by Charles Taylor's forces from the government forces. The only minor difference was that it was dark and that we did not have to grab travel bags to run to an unknown destination. I felt like my worst nightmare had come to reality. This time I felt my heart pounding because of anxiety. The first time I encountered Charles Taylor's force, I accepted them with gladness. I, like many others, were ignorant and believed that they were liberators. However, we quickly found out how wicked they were. Now we wanted no part of them. Anyway, we all ran out of our home. When we arrived outside, I noticed that other neighbors were outside with their families as well. We all seemed to be running around in distress. I quickly learned that Charles Taylor's forces had started to shell the city again. We were all waiting outside to run away from the missile and survive the shelling. While I was outside, I heard a whistling sound. I knew what it was, and I looked in the direction of the whistling sound. I saw a small flame soaring through the night air. I was no military expert, but I assumed that it was a missile. The missile was flying very high. My father and the other men in the neighborhood quickly realized that the missile was flying too high to come down on us. Therefore, they instructed everyone to run toward the missile, assuming that the missile would fly over us to a further destination. We all ran underneath the missile in the opposite direction. By the grace of God, the missile did indeed fly over us without striking us and exploding. Not too long after we evaded the missile, we heard a loud explosion. I could not help but imagine the possibility that I could have been harmed by that missile attack. I also prayed in my heart that no one would be injured or killed by that missile. The initial missile attack was followed by several more missile attacks. The sound of each missile explosion was devastating because it created the opportunity for destruction to homes or could result in injury or death. The missile attack lasted for approximately thirty minutes, but it seemed like it lasted for several hours. Even after the shelling stopped, we stayed outdoors because we did not know what to expect. We were at the mercy of wicked individuals whose intention was to destroy us. However, I believe that God protected us and kept us safe from those wicked individuals. That night, as we all returned inside our homes, I was relieved that I was not recaptured by Charles Taylor's forces. I also learned that the darkness created a better opportunity for us to see the missile and get away from it. This was very important because during daylight we could not see the missile, we could only hear it.

The following morning I woke up to learn that many of the missiles fell into the Atlantic Ocean. I also learned that at least one of the missiles fell on land and damaged a home.

That day I stayed glued to the radio to learn more about what was going on. I also heard gun firing in the outskirts of the city of Monrovia. Sometimes the gunfire was light, and at other times, they were very heavy. We did our best as children to keep ourselves occupied. Since school was closed, we spent a lot of time playing basketball and tennis with our friends in our neighborhood. We always stayed close to home because the time was very uncertain. Although I continuously prayed for the ECOMOG peacekeepers to successfully protect us and defeat Charles Taylor's forces, I also anticipated a possible infiltration by Charles Taylor's force.

The missile attack continued for a few more days. The experience was more difficult during the daylight. The missiles were concealed by the daylight. All that we had to indicate the location of the missile was the whistling sound. Nevertheless, at times the whistling sound was a bit too late. However, by the grace of God, we were not injured. Eventually, my father was able to allow us to use his office to sleep during the night. It was perfect for the conditions at hand. My father's office was located on the ground floor in the middle of the hospital. Therefore, any impact from the missile explosion would, at best, be indirect. So we slept in my father's office to protect ourselves from Charles Taylor's missile attack. Charles Taylor's attack lead many to become anxious, and they decided to flee Monrovia. So many people were looking for a way out of Monrovia. Most planes had stopped flying into Monrovia. Liberians seemed to have moved from a country motivated by love of liberty to a country fueled by anger. It made no sense why people who should have had so much love and support for one another would tear each other apart so maliciously. However, we had allowed anger and pain to develop in us to the extent that we had become like barbarians to each other.

As the fighting continued, I received a devastating news in the early stages of the attack. One day, I was listening to *BBC News*, it was reported that several Catholic missionaries were murdered in Gardnerville, which is located on the outskirts of Monrovia. This news had a profound impact on me and my community. My father worked in a Catholic organization, and my family also resided in a community with a heavy influence from the Catholic organization. Both the St. Joseph Catholic Hospital and the S. M. A. Father's guesthouse were in my neighborhood. I was also saddened when I learned that my school principal and one of my school staff members were identified as some of the missionaries that had been murdered by members of Charles Taylor's NPFL forces. The rumor was that they were intentionally murdered. I had grown to become very fond of Sister Shirley Kolmer and Sister Barbara Muttra. These two individuals certainly had an impact in my life, and I appreciated all that they did to build my foundation. Sister Shirley was very instrumental in getting me to attend St. Patrick's High School, which was considered one of the best schools in Liberia. While I had the opportunity to attend St. Patrick's High School, I lacked the confidence to even apply for attendance there. Sister Shirley gave me the confidence that I needed to apply myself. I learned to apply myself not only to St. Patrick's High School, but also to the challenges that I would face in my life. Sister Barbara influenced my life in a different way. She was more of a no-nonsense disciplinarian. While she was not one of my regular teachers, she was always around, checking on us to see if we were doing what we were supposed to be doing. She was particularly active in my class. I believed that she spend so much time with us because we were new and she wanted to install the culture and expectation of the school in us. We were all new to an all-male school because this was the only school of its kind in Liberia at the time. We were also very different, with so many differences in our personalities. Therefore, we had to learn to come together as a unit. Sister Barbara understood that unity was key to our success at St. Patrick's High School, and she was trying to guide us into achieving that. In hindsight, I can say that she did accomplish her goal because the relationships that I formed at St. Patrick's High School are still active today. Her method of disciplining us left an even memorable impact on me. Sister Barbara was very witty. She always seemed to have a quick response to those who attempted to bully her or get one over on her. While she often responded with words, she also sometimes responded with punishments that would lead to a period of ridicule from your classmates. I certainly did not want to be ridiculed by my peers; they were pretty brutal. I did not want that kind of attention; no one did. Therefore, most of the boys in my class chose not to play silly games with her. The murder of the five Catholic nuns affected so many Liberians because many Liberians were positively impacted by them. Their legacy will continue to be felt in Liberia.

By the grace of God, the ECOMOG peacekeepers started to gain an advantage on the battlefield. This was largely made possible by the fighter jets (Doo-Doo Boy) that brought terror and fear among Charles Taylor's force. Fortunately, with the availability of the fighter jets, the peacekeepers were able to make some major advances to push Charles Taylor's rebel forces away from Monrovia. I remembered watching the ECOMOG fighter jet in action on several occasions as they attacked and defeated Charles Taylor's forces. Those fighter pilots were amazing. Their tactical maneuvers were pretty spectacular. One of the maneuvers that I most admired was the pilot flying the jet high into the sky. Then the pilot would turn the engine off so that the enemies could not hear the sound of the jet approaching. The jet would fall from the sky at a very high speed as if it was falling out of control. To best describe the maneuver, it was very similar to an eagle attacking its prey. When the fighter jets came down low enough to Charles Taylor's forces, it would deploy its explosives and destroy members of Charles Taylor's forces. The fighter jet would then fly away in a spinning motion at a high rate of speed. Usually, the jet would have completed its mission and be on its way out before the sound of the explosive could be heard. I always wondered how a person could do all those maneuvers without becoming lightheaded. However, they did it, I was simply glad that they were on my side and not Charles Taylor's. I remember that I had a real scare one day when I heard that Charles Taylor had acquired a fighter jet. I was playing basketball with my brothers and neighborhood friends when I saw a fighter jet flying by. Shortly after seeing the first jet flying by, we observed a second jet flying by at a high rate of speed. It was so noticeable that we all stated to wonder what going on. It was at this time that someone mentioned that the first jet belonged to Charles Taylor's forces while the second jet was an ECOMOG peace-keeper jet chasing after Charles Taylor's jet. When I heard that news, my heart sunk to my stomach. I did not want to imagine what life would become if Charles Taylor and his forces acquired a fighter jet in his arsenal. In hindsight, we were all simply afraid. We really did not know what was happening, and we were simply anticipating the worse. Fortunately for us, Charles Taylor did not possess a fighter jet. What we likely witness was one ECOMOG jet attempting to catch up with another ECOMOG fighter jet.

With nothing to do, I continued to spend more time playing basketball with my neighborhood friends. During this time, Brother Jose started to teach us how to play tennis. Brother Jose loved tennis, and he attempted to keep us occupy through the game of tennis. It was an excellent way to get our minds off the war and to also learn something new. He certainly succeeded in teaching us the game of tennis. Not only did we learn the game of tennis, but also many of us continued to play tennis even until this day. However, the state of our reality was too overwhelming for us to take our minds off the war for too long of a period. I was grateful for an opportunity to get my mind off the sounds of gun firing and missiles exploding.

The war continued for a few more months. Eventually, a peace agreement was established between Charles Taylor and ECOWAS, and the fighting ended. It was a period of joy and celebration. At the end of the year, a large extravagant party was held for the senior staff by the Brothers and Sisters from the St. Joseph Catholic Hospital. I fondly remember this moment because it was nothing like I had ever experienced. We had a feast in an opened beautiful garden in the rear of the Brothers' residence. Food was unlimited. There, I got my first experience drinking sangria. It had to be the best drink I had. Although I was only a teenager, I was able to drink alcoholic drink. It was not illegal to consume alcoholic beverage at the time. It was up to the discretion of the parent or guardian to make that decision. My father certainly did not allow me to consume alcoholic beverage regularly. However, given the moment, he allowed us to participate in consuming the drink. I did not become intoxicated; therefore, I believe that if any alcohol was included in our drink it was likely very minimum. The party lasted most of the night. We had such great time after the party that it became a thing at the end of every year. I, along with other kids that resided at the location, looked forward to the elaborate end-of-the-year Christmas party held in the beautiful open garden.

Personal Battles

After the peace agreement was established, I was a little hesitant. The fact is I, like many others in Monrovia, were skeptical because of Charles Taylor's history regarding following peace agreements. Prior to this peace agreement, Charles Taylor had disregarded several other peace agreements. Therefore, we all had reasons to be uncertain about the peace agreement that had just passed. Was this agreement another strategy for Charles Taylor to replenish his arsenal and manpower for a subsequent attack? I certainly hope not. This cycle of war was draining life out of me. However, all that I could do was trust and hope in God that the peace agreement would be honored by Charles Taylor. Everyone was happy that the fighting had stopped and that Charles Taylor was not successful in overtaking Monrovia. Had he been successful, I believe that my chance of survival would have been greatly reduced. Government offices, local businesses, and other institutions such as churches started to reopen. The recreational location located at ACS (American Corporation School) also reopened. I was really glad when it reopened because I really needed a break from all the stress that was created as a result of the fighting. I was able to return to my favorite hobbies of playing basketball and hanging out with my friends. While I was taking full advantage of the freedom that I was given, I was also very mindful to stay away from the outskirts of the city. I certainly did not want to be in an area where Charles Taylor's forces could likely attack and cause me to become separated from my family.

As the security of Monrovia became stable, schools reopened. My school, St. Patrick's High School, also reopened. I was excited to return to school to see friends that I was disconnected from for several months and to also continue my education. My return to school was a bittersweet experience. There was a kind of tension in the air, an elephant in the room. School did not feel the same without the presence of our principal Sister Shirley Kolmer and Sister Barbara. It felt like something had been taken from me. Many of my schoolmates expressed the same feeling. However, loss had become very familiar to me as a result of the civil war. So I did what I knew that I should do. I had to keep moving forward. Nothing could be done to bring back what was lost.

As time went by, things got much better. My paternal grandmother was finally able to become liberated from her home, which was within Charles Taylor's territory, and come to my home. I was just beginning to experience life as a teenager, and I must say it was one of the best times of my life. In spite of living in a nation with an ongoing civil war, I found ways to enjoy my teenage life. School was a lot of fun in spite of the hard work that I had to put into being successful in my education. I enjoyed hanging out with my friends from the neighborhood, playing basketball and tennis. Although I enjoyed both sports, I was more fond of basketball. As my life seemed to be getting on the right path, I came across a bump in the road. Not too long after returning to school, I developed an illness that would last for most of my teenage life. It all began during a basketball game that I was participating in. As I was sitting on the bench as a substitute, I passed out. I really do not recall what happened after that. When I regained consciousness, I noticed that I was in an ambulance. I attempted to get up because I was confused. I did not know what was going on. However, I was restrained, and I could not get up. I was only able to lift my head up enough to see my father driving his work vehicle, which was a red Chevrolet sedan. Seeing my father helped to calm my confused state of mind. I knew that my father was aware of whatever was going on. I was taken to the St. Joseph Catholic Hospital, and I was immediately taken to the emergency room for treatment. I later learned that I had an epileptic episode as a result of a very high fever. I was informed that the fever was so high that it could have affected my brain. I also received stitches on my ears because it tore apart while I was fighting and kicking around on the cement basketball court during my epileptic episode. I was admitted to the hospital for a few days before I was released to return home. My brothers and neighbors later stopped by to visit me. During this time, they informed me how I passed out and started fighting uncontrollably on the basketball court. They also informed me that they were scared because of my behavior and they did not know what to do. This would be the beginning of many years of illness that I would deal with. I was later informed that I had become ill with malaria. When I heard this, I was a bit confused. I had lived in Liberia all my life, and malaria had not caused me to have seizures. So, I wondered how malaria was now having such a drastic impact on my health. I was provided with some of the best medical treatment that I could have received in Monrovia during that time. However, the illness kept returning every year. I was admitted into the hospital at least twice a year. I would experience high fever with a temperature of approximately 105 degrees quite often. It was a very difficult period in my life. A few times my schooling was obstructed because of my illness. I was sometimes so weak that I would be walking and abruptly fall unconscious. I vividly recall one of such incidents where I was walking in the kitchen and I started to lose consciousness. As I was falling to the kitchen floor, my father saw me and caught me before I hit the floor. Luckily, my father was there at the right time to protect me from causing further injury to myself. There was a large wooden table in the kitchen, and I likely would have struck my head on the table had my father not being there. I experienced many more incidents like this during the remainder of my stay in Liberia.

By the grace of God, I continued to carry my weight in spite of my illness. I still continued to maintain my grades at school. I still went to fetch water rolling those large heavy barrels of water. During this time, my father also taught my brothers and me how to cook. According to my father, he wanted us to be independent. He always stated, "I don't want any woman to bluff you." I continued to remain active in sports, playing basketball and tennis. In spite of my challenges, I learned how to persevere. I felt like I had already wasted enough time staying out of school as a result of the civil war. I did not want to be held back any longer in my education, and I definitely did not want my childhood to be stolen from me. If there was any fun to be had, I wanted to be a part of it. So I did exactly that.

I am forever grateful that I made the decision to persevere instead of allowing my circumstances to get the best of me. It was during this time that I learned a very important lesson. While trying to stay active and have fun as a teenager, I decided to sign up for the YMCA basketball summer league. During my attempt, I played in the junior varsity basketball league. During that tournament, I worked hard, doing all that I could to get my team to win the tournament. I was not a good scorer. So I had to quickly figure out what my skills were. I quickly learned to use my high level of athleticism to be a defensive nightmare. At the end of the tournament, I won the award for the highest steal, highest block, and highest rebound. While I was proud of my personal accomplishments in the tournament, I felt that I could do more. I felt that I could win a championship. It was a personal goal of mine to win a championship in the next tournament. Although I was eager to play in the next tournament, I had to patiently wait for the following summer to have another opportunity to compete for the title. I took the opportunity to develop my skills off the court. I began to increase my vertical leap, and I learned to dunk the basketball into the hoop. My hard work eventually led me to become the captain of my class basketball team.

By the following summer basketball tournament, I felt like I was ready to go and accomplish my goal. I went and signed up for the varsity league. I had just turned sixteen years old and made the cut to move up to the "big" league. So I signed up, not knowing who my teammates were going to be. This was the way that it was done, the players were supposed to be selected randomly so that the selection process could be fair. I would later find out who my teammates would be. I was really hoping for a team with really good players. That would definitely increase my odds of accomplishing my goal of winning the tournament. The list was eventually posted. After the teams were selected, I was really disappointed. I had come to discover that three of the teams in the league were stacked with the best high school players in the nation. I had observed all of those guys play in games to know how good they were. They were far better than I was. Those players had the skills, confidence, and experience that I lacked. As for my team, only three players on my team could effectively dribble the ball, and I was one of the three. The other players were my neighbor Jimi. The third player was Ricky. I did not know Ricky very well, but I quickly discovered during practice that he was a scoring machine. Okay, so we now had a decent scorer. Ricky was very fast and good at making layups. Jimi was an okay shot blocker and rebounder. We also had one half decent player who was approximately 6'1"; he was an average center. I was appointed the team captain, and I was assigned to play defense. My coach, Coach Borbor, was my previous coach; and he was familiar with me. I believe that Coach Borbor saw something in me that made him believe that I would make a good team captain. Frankly, after comparing my team to the other teams, winning the tournament was my least concern. I could only hope that my team would not be the first team to be kicked out.

However, as the team captain, I continued to encourage my teammates, especially Ricky and Jimi. I encouraged Ricky and Jimi more because I knew that the bulk of the work depended on the three of us. I wanted them to be prepared to play a lot of minutes during all our games. It seemed like this tournament was going to be more work than fun. Meanwhile, the other competitive teams had at least two stars on their team and the supporting players were also much better than Jimi and me. I thought that the selection process was not fair. In fact, I strongly believed that it was staged. I believed that the organizers wanted a good show and that they selected purposefully for that reason.

For my first game, I played against a team that included two of the best players from my school. That was bad news for my team because these two players also happened to be the best duo in the nation. This team also happened to include players who were on the starting five from schools with excellent basketball programs. During my first game, my team lost in such an embarrassing manner that I just wanted to disappear off the court. My team became a laughingstock that day. While it was largely expected that my team would lose the game, we were ridiculed to the extreme. I became so upset at the amount of ridicule that my teammates and I received that I made a promise to meet and defeat that team later. I continued to lead my team, encouraging my teammates to do their best. I was determined to win, and I played my best every game. Although I was not the best player on the team, my efforts encouraged the other players on my team to also do their best. Collectively, my team improved, and we started to win games. We won consecutive games after our initial loss. Before I knew it, my team had made it to the quarterfinals. Without realizing it, we had defeated most of those teams that we were concerned about.

Our story caught the attention of the local news, and an article was written in the local newspaper. I must say that I was very excited that my team made the newspaper. I was even more excited that my name and those of my teammates made the newspaper. My team had an amazing story because it came from being an underdog to defeating teams with better players. While we had a few easy wins, majority of our games were tough battles. With the recognition and attention that my team was getting, other players started to play against my teammates and me more aggressively. In fact, I remembered attempting to play a game of pickup basketball with a childhood friend of mine, and he intentionally tripped me. It was like he was intentionally trying to injure me so that I was unable to play the next game, which happened to be the semifinals. It then became very real to me how even my friends were opposed to me winning the tournament. I get it that I played a role in defeating them. However, I did not realize that they would become malicious and attempt to sabotage me by injuring me. I now knew to be careful and protect myself until the tournament concluded. With the exception of team practices, I stayed away from pickup basketball games. Even when I stayed away from playing pickup games with my friends, I was still harassed by my friends about the tournament. I understood the harassment because we were very competitive. Also some of my friends had siblings and other relatives on the teams that I was scheduled to play against. I personally believe that the culture in Liberia largely influenced the response of some of my peers.

Liberia has a culture of discouraging one another instead of supporting others. It was the norm to ridicule others, especially in school. The term *voke*, which is derived from the word *provoke*, was often used by Liberians around me. Ridiculing others was a way of life in Liberia. However, I chose to remain focused on achieving my goal. I played in the semifinals, and my team won the game. I was now at the finish line. I just needed to cross the finish line. After the semifinals, we were given a week break to rest and prepare for the final game. Although I was eager, I had to play the waiting game. During this time, I had to deal with more harassment from my peers who openly showed their disdain because my teammates and I had made it to the finals. So many times I heard the "Who do you think you are?" and "Do you really think that you're going to win?" comments. I chose not to engage those who wanted to argue with me about who was going to win or lose. I decided to simply show them who would win by actually winning the final game.

In the finals, I was going against two of the best players in my school. These guys happened to be playing on the team that my team lost to in the initial game. As I saw it, I had another opportunity to defeat this team. I had built up enough confidence, and I believed that I could defeat this team. Although I was confident, I knew that this was going to be a huge challenge. My opponent had not lost a single game during the tournament. They were the favorite to win the tournament. I believed that they were not too concerned about losing to my team. After all, they defeated my team in the past. To make things even more challenging, I was also dealing with malaria. I had been dealing with malaria during the tournament. Sometimes, I was unable to fully participate due to my illness. I felt weak, like I was about to pass out. However, I continue to strive as I participated in the tournament. I was determined to complete the tournament, even win it. I was hoping that my illness would stay away and allow me to fully participate in the final game.

Unfortunately, the day prior to the final game, I fell ill. I started to feel down because I felt like I would be unable to do my best. I was a little concerned that I might become ill to the point of being unable to play the game. I really wanted to play in the final game, even if I could not be my best self. The day of the game I felt good enough to play. My father was very concerned; however, he allowed me to make the decision to play. When the game started, I decided to put all my effort into the game. I played aggressively because I did not want to lose to this team again. My opponents also played aggressively. They had a reputation to uphold, and they were not willing to lose it to a bunch of nobodies. We all played with high intensity, and the game ended with a tie. During the game I had to sit out a few times due to my illness. Several of the league officials even questioned if I should be allowed to continue playing in the game. I resisted the idea and continued to participate. After the game ended, I felt like giving up because I felt so bad. Not only was I fatigue from playing with such high intensity, I was also dealing with the effects of the malaria. My temperature was so high that my breath felt like heat. I also felt weakness to the extent that I was going to lose consciousness. Coach Borbor insisted that I stay out of the game. However, I had gotten this far, and I did not want my efforts to go in vain. So I agreed to sit out at the beginning of the overtime game. It did take long for me to notice that I was needed back into the game. Our opponents were benefiting from my absence. I brought defense to the team. Without my defense, the scorers on the other team started to have their way. This time Coach Borbor did not object. I was in the game, and I played with all of my energy. Eventually, my team was able to catch up, and the overtime ended with a tie again. After the overtime game ended, I felt like I could not breathe. I was hot from fever, my heart felt like it was about to stop, and I started to believe that I was going to pass out. Even my teammates were starting to encourage me to stay out of the game. I initially entertained the idea, and I lay on the bench for a while. As the second overtime game was about to start, I started to feel a little better. I was able to breathe, and I no longer felt like I was going to lose consciousness. I told Coach Borbor that I was ready to get back into the game. I knew that this would probably be our last chance, and I did not want to miss out on the action. I started the second overtime game. Initially, we were all aggressive on the court. However, I started to notice that our opponents started to play less aggressively. At this time, I realized that the fatigue of the game had caught up to them. My teammates also realized the fatigue factor in our opponents and became encouraged. I became encouraged and played my defensive position more aggressively. Although the effects of my illness were creating a real challenge for me, I continued to persevere. When it was clear that my team would win the game, Coach Borbor pulled me out. The game ended with my team winning the tournament and landing our opponents their first defeat. They also happened to be the only team that defeated us. It was such a good feeling to pay back and defeat the only team that defeated us. Like the saying goes, "He who laugh last, laughs the best." I also got to shut up all of my peers who harassed me and attempted to discourage me by attempting to put doubt in my mind about winning the tournament. This experience taught me some of the most important lessons in my life. Through my experience in the tournament, I learned to exercise confidence, I learned to persevere, and I learned to overcome. What I experienced in this tournament left a lasting positive impact in my life.

The Return of One Liberia

As I continued to exist in an uncertain Liberia, there was a consistent effort by the international community to reunite the nation. One of the ways that this would be accomplished was to allow the different warring factions to come together to form a single government. I was excited, like many other Liberians. This merger could possibly create an opportunity for the nation to be reunited again and end the civil war. After a lengthy period of negotiating, the agreement was finalized. A single government was formed comprising of members from each key party involved in the civil war. This was exciting times in Liberia. On the day that the different groups came into Monrovia, people lined up the major streets to welcome their fellow Liberians. The convoys from all of various parties paraded into Monrovia. It was amazing to see how Liberians quickly put away their bitterness and pain for a chance to reunite with their fellow Liberians in spite of the offenses committed against them by these various warring factions. Beneath the pain was the need to live in peace and love one another. This was a reflection of 1 Corinthians 13:7 (ESV), which states that "Love bears all things, believe all things, hopes all things, endures all things." I got to see the power of love. Love is indeed a powerful thing. The various convoys drove through Monrovia and attended a program that was hosted to welcome them into Monrovia. The plan for the new government was to work together until a free and fair election was held. However, the various warring factions would continue to maintain control of their captured territories until the election was held. Also, the ECOMOG peacekeepers would also continue to maintain security in Monrovia until the election was held and security was stabilized.

During this period, there were some ups and downs. The different groups always did not agree. There were times where there were treats of fights breaking up between the different groups in Monrovia. These treats always worried me because I did not want to experience the terrors that I went through again. One day, I came to face that fear. I was visiting a friend on a typical hot afternoon in the Congo Town area when I started to hear rapid gunfire. I did not know what was going on and neither did the friend who I was visiting. My friend Clinton wanted me to stay until the shooting had ceased. However, I did not want to relive the trauma of being separated from my family like my mother had become. That would have been too much for my father to deal with. He had already lost his wife and his brother-in-law, who was like a son to him. Losing me would have created more problems for my father. Therefore, I made the decision to run home. Although it was a big risk, I believed that the shooting had just started, and I had a small window of opportunity to return home. My strategy was to return home before the fighting escalated. As I was running home, I learned that the shooting might have been occurring around Charles Taylor's headquarter located in Congo Town. Charles Taylor's headquarter was on the most direct route that led to my home. That meant I would have to run into danger if I was going to take the quickest route home. I was desperate; therefore, I decided to take the direct route while hoping that the fighting ceased prior to me getting there. So I ran at full speed, in my attempt to get home safely. However, as I was approaching Charles Taylor's headquarter, the sound of the shooting increased. I made the decision to take an alternate route, which made my journey longer. I was afraid about prolonging my return home. However, I did not want my father to discover that I wasn't home. I rather return home safely and deal with my father's anger later. By the grace of God, I made it home safely. My father had not returned home. Therefore, I was not in any trouble. I did not have to deal with hearing my father's complaints regarding me visiting friends and risking my safety.

During this period of the transitional government, it became quite apparent that Charles Taylor's NPFL organization had the most influence among all the other warring factions. Not only did he have high influence within the transitional government, but he surprisingly also had strong support among many Liberians. This was true among many younger Liberians. Many Liberians, especially the youths, idolized Charles Taylor because he represented success and power. Charles Taylor provided cars and wealth for his close associates. His officials often flaunted their wealth, which, by the way, was wealth gained by confiscating the nation's wealth for personal gains. Let's not forget the terror that he had brought upon the people of Liberia. I could not understand how the people of Liberia could've quickly forgotten how Charles Taylor and members of his organization committed so many acts of violence against the people of Liberia. I often found myself wondering if the people of Liberia had truly forgiven Charles Taylor so quickly or if they were just simply naive. As for me, the only reasonable explanation that I could accept was that the Liberian people felt the need to support Charles Taylor in order to avoid more fighting. I was certain about one thing: I did not believe that Charles Taylor had repented for his actions. In fact, he and his members were still committing acts of terror against the Liberian people. Therefore, I was not going to be carried away by wealth obtained through theft of Liberia's resources.

I was truly angry at my fellow Liberians because of the support that they were giving to Charles Taylor. It almost seemed like he had a magic wand that he was using to hypnotize his supporters. I really could not understand how the response of so many Liberians could be possible. After pondering this matter for a period, I realized that I could do nothing about it. At some point during this period, I realized that anger was consuming me. I did not know who to place my anger against. Was I supposed to be angry at Charles Taylor? Well, that was understandable considering the problems that Charles Taylor had caused in Liberia. But how could I be angry at the people of Liberia. Many of them experienced some of the same atrocities that I had experienced. So not only was I angry, I was also confused. I simply could not comprehend any valid reason why so many Liberians would support Charles Taylor. When I could no longer carry on with the angry and confusion, I turned to God for help. Since I did not know how to overcome my anger and confusion, I figured God could help me overcome that burden. "Come to me all who labor and are heavy laden and I will give you rest" (Matt. 11:28 ESV). I learned in Sunday school that I could turn to God whenever I had a problem and that God would help me overcome that problem. So I started becoming more attentive in church. Now I had a reason to seek God. I did not only attend church out of expectation, I also started to attend weekly Bible study. I liked Bible study because I could ask questions and gain more understanding of the Bible. I certainly learned some biblical principles. Most importantly, I learned how to apply those biblical principles to my personal life. Applying those biblical principles to my personal life certainly had a positive impact in my life. I learned to see the crucifixion of Jesus in a whole new way. It was no longer just a Bible story. I now saw the pain and suffering that Jesus endure on the cross from a different perspective. In spite of all that Jesus endured, he still forgave those who betrayed him and falsely prosecuted him. Therefore, I learned that I too had to forgive those who I felt offended by, including Charles Taylor and those who supported him. I also learned that I was born as a sinner and that my sins would not be forgiven if I don't forgive others. "But if you do not forgive others their trespasses, neither will your Father forgive your trespasses" (Matt. 6:15 ESV).

Once I got to understand that the forgiveness of my sin depended upon me forgiving others, I understood why I had to let my anger go. After all, Jesus endured much more pain than I did, and yet he forgave. Therefore, I knew that I had to forgive even Charles Taylor and all those politicians and soldiers who played a role in separating my mother from my family. I was still confused at the time as to why so many Liberians like myself would support Charles Taylor after he had caused so much pain and suffering to Liberia and its people. However, there was not much that I could do about why the others made the decisions that they did. I was able to accomplish forgivingness through the strength of God. When I leaned on God for strength during the forgiveness process, I seemed to gain wisdom that brought the understanding that I needed to forgive. When I forgive those who had caused me pain, I had peace in my mind and peace in my heart. I stopped worrying about Charles Taylor and why the people of Liberia were supporting him after what he had done. I started to focus on my future. I knew that I wanted a future where I could live in a peaceful environment and successfully provide for myself. While I really wanted to be able to live a successful and peaceful life in Liberia, I realized that that it might not be possible. Not in a Liberia where Charles Taylor could eventually become the leader of the nation. I also perceived that if Charles Taylor was to become president of Liberia, Liberia would eventually be in a state of chaos. I already experienced what Liberia was like under his leadership. I also believed that war would have returned to Liberia under a President Taylor because of all the groups that he had wronged. Therefore, I started to look for a way out of Liberia. Unfortunately, I did not have a suitable place that I could flee to. While I had relatives in the United States and Europe, I had no communication with them. So they really could not help me and my family at the time. With nowhere to go and no one to turn to, I decided to turn to God once more to make a way for my family. I believed that God could make a way for us although we had no foreseeable way out of Liberia. I had come to learn that God hears us when we call on him. I also learned that whatever I ask in God's name that he would do it (John 14:14 ESV). So I went to God with a new burden. I asked God to bless my family and get us out of Liberia before it was too late. I did not want to be in Liberia if Charles Taylor became president. While there was no guarantee that Charles Taylor would have won the election, he seemed to be the favorite presidential candidate to win the election. I prayed fervently, asking God to make a way for my family to leave Liberia, and I believed that God would make a way. I did not know what means God would use to get my family out of Liberia, but I had faith knowing that God would answer my prayers.

(Photos from the 90's in Monrovia)

(Photos from the 90's in Monrovia)

(Photos from the 90's in Monrovia)

(Photos from the 90's in Monrovia)

Hope Arrives

I continued to get more involved with the church, and I started to grow in my faith. As I continued growing in my faith, I became more at peace with myself. I stopped worrying about why many Liberians favored Charles Taylor and allowed him to manipulate them. I also became noticeably calmer in my behavior. I observed that I was not as aggressive as I used to be. While I was not a troublesome child, I did not run away from fights. I was a strong believer of standing my ground, and if it meant getting into physical fights, I was okay with that. I felt really good existing in this peaceful state.

As I continued to seek God, I continued to look for opportunities to get out of Liberia. I happened to have had several friends who could be evacuated out of Liberia at a moment's notice if fighting broke out in Monrovia. I wanted the same opportunities as well, especially if Charles Taylor was going to win the presidential election. As I was waiting on God for an answer to my prayer, I received a response from God. In 1996 while at school, my close friend told me about a diversity visa lottery program to travel to the United States. I really did not understand what he was telling me. It did not make any sense to me. My initial thought was, *Will the United States government really provide an opportunity for anyone to travel to United States?* I questioned the opportunity because I knew that so many people wanted to come to the United States. I would think that the government would have been overwhelmed. So it did not make sense to me that the United States government would want to create more work for themselves. I eventually learned that this was a legitimate program that was created by the United States government. The program, which was also referred to as the green card lottery, provided United States permanent resident immigration to those whose applications were picked. It was basically like playing the lottery. I believed that everyone had a fair chance to win because the program was not ran by corrupt Liberian officials. I immediately thought that this was God's answer to my prayer. This was exactly what I was looking for. I wanted to leave Liberia, and my first choice of countries to travel to was the United States. During that time, I saw the United States as a safe haven, and also, there were so many interesting things about the United States. I knew that travelling to America would give me the opportunity to escape the dangers of living in Liberia and live in a country that I considered the greatest nation on earth.

So I went home and told my brothers about the diversity visa lottery program. I knew that I had to get them to buy into the idea before I could make this proposal to my father. My father held two significant positions at both places of his employment. He also owned his own successful business. He would have to give up a whole lot to travel to the United States. He would be giving up certainty for uncertainty regarding his career by traveling to the United States. So I needed my brothers' support. It did not take much to convince my brothers. Everyone I knew wanted to travel to or reside in the United States. Once they realized that we had a chance, they were sold. After gaining the support of my brothers, I told my father about the diversity visa lottery program, which was also known as DV-97. At first, my father was hesitant because he too did not know that such a program existed. However, once he realized that the programs was legitimate, he agreed to complete the application on behalf of our family. My father understood the implications that such opportunity would have on the future of my brothers and me. Therefore, he chose to forfeit his successful careers to give us a better future. Initially, my father did not complete the application. He was probably very busy since he worked two jobs. I certainly understood his position; however, I did not want us to miss the deadline for submitting the application. So I rallied my brothers to make frequent inquiries about the completion of the application form. I was 100 percent certain that this was God's answer to my prayer to leave Liberia, and I did not want us to miss God's blessing. Once my father realized that we would not stop bothering him until the form was completed, he started working to complete the form. The form was very lengthy, but he worked on it whenever he had time to spare. Eventually, my father completed and submitted the form.

I felt so relieved when he informed me that the form had been submitted. I had faith and believed that God was going to do his part now that we had done what we needed to do. All that we needed to do was to wait for the results to come out. At first, I was filled with anxiety. However, the selection process took a long time. I eventually grew tired of being anxious.

Unfortunately, challenges always seemed to present themselves in Liberia. It did not take long before tension started to rise in Monrovia between two of the parties. The tension certainly got my mind off being anxious about the result of the diversity visa lottery. The tension brought about uncertainty. One morning, I was on the bus going to school when I learned that schools had been closed. Since I was catching a ride on the employee bus for the St. Joseph Catholic Hospital, I continued riding on the bus. The bus had to pick up employees from around the city of Monrovia. As the bus continued to travel through the city, picking up employees, we came to Broad Street, near the YMCA. I was familiar with this area because I often played basketball at the YMCA. At this location, we came upon a checkpoint. I knew that this was bad news. Suddenly, a soldier wearing a solid-green military uniform appeared. His uniform indicated that he was a member of the Armed Forces of Liberia (AFL), which was loyal to the late President Doe. Without saying a word, I knew that he did not want us there. The soldier slowly walked toward the bus pointing his rifle to the bus. He soldier spoke with the driver very briefly, and then he shouted instructions for the driver to get out of the area. The soldier's command was immediately followed by the sound of gunfire. The bus driver reversed so quickly that I feared that he would drive off the road. Fortunately, the bus stayed on the road, and the bus driver returned us home safely. This was a very scary encounter for me because it brought back the fear of being separated from my family. Of course, such encounters always reminded me of how my mother was forcibly separated from her family. This encounter also reinforced my desire to want to leave Liberia. Liberia was simply not stable. There was lack of security, and a gunfight could occur at any moment. I continued to pray for God's protection while also praying for God to protect my family. Tough circumstances also motivate one to pray, especially when you have no other way out of your circumstance, I did not want another fight to occur. This could cost my family's opportunity to migrate to the United States to be missed. During fighting, people often relocate. The poor method of communication would have greatly hindered the diversity visa lottery process. I really did not want to lose such great opportunity. Therefore, I became anxious again. I was so worried that I became afraid. I started to ask myself what if there is a major fight and we lose the opportunity to migrate to the United States. I couldn't imagine how I would feel if that occur. So I decided to focus on reading my Bible and getting closer to God. This would be a better option than worrying myself about something that I had no control over. I also continued to work on maintaining an even balance in my life. I did the best that I could in school. I also continued playing basketball and tennis while enjoying hanging out with friends. In spite of all of the challenges that existed in Liberia at the time, I found ways to have fun. However, I was cautious not to allow the fun to overshadow my expectations in school.

One afternoon, I stayed after school for basketball practice. After basketball practice, my father showed up at my school and picked me up. This was not unusual; however, it was not expected. I went with my father. I was always happy when he picked me up. Catching a cab in Monrovia could be difficult. Often, one literally had to fight to catch a cab. This was one day that I did not have to fight to catch a cab. While driving home from school, I noticed that my father was quiet. I became concerned. I thought I had gotten into some kind of trouble. I just could not figure out what I had done to get into trouble. So I attempted to initiate a conversation to get a clue about what my father was thinking. My father did not really say anything that indicated that I was in trouble. When I arrived home, my father simply dropped me off and instructed me to tell my brothers to meet him in his office. At this time, I was certain that my brothers and I were in trouble. Now I was wondering what we had done. I could not think of anything in particular. However, I informed my brothers about my father's instruction. So we all went to meet my father at the hospital in his office. When we arrived at my father's office, I noticed that he appeared happy. That was a sign that perhaps my father was not upset. With a big smile on his face, he told us to sit down. Then he said, "Gentlemen, I got good news." I wanted to believe that the results of the diversity visa lottery had become available; however, I did not want to get myself too excited. My father did confirm that the results had been made known. My father informed us that someone who had played the diversity lottery went to check on the result and they noticed that my father's name was on the list. Unfortunately, my father's friend did not see his name on the list. At that moment, I became overwhelmed with excitement. My brothers and I were jumping for joy. We did our best to contain our excitement since we were in my father's office. Then my father informed us that he had to stop by the United States embassy to confirm the results. While the news was great, the result still needed to be confirmed. It was possible that the information could have been wrong. The names of those who were selected were posted on the wall outside of the United States embassy in Mamba Point. Hundreds of people would travel to the United States embassy to search the list for their names. Many left heartbroken. I could only wish that my father's friend was right and that we too would not become heartbroken.

I tried to hold in my excited until the information could be confirmed. The next day I went to school with a high level of anxiety. I believed within myself that God had already answered my prayer. However, I was still anxious and excited at the same time. After school, I was anxiously waiting on the confirmation from my father. He did not return home until he got off work at 5:00 p.m. It seemed like it took forever for my father to return home.

While hanging out on the back porch with my brothers, I saw my father walking home from the hospital. As he got closer to the house, I saw a smile on his face. At this point, I had all the confirmation that I needed. When my father arrived home, he informed my brothers and me that he went to the United States embassy and confirmed that his name was listed on the wall. Now I could display my excitement freely. This meant that my family had won visas to travel to the United States. Obtaining a visa to travel to America can be almost impossible. Therefore, this was a blessing. We were going to travel to the United States on a permanent resident status. This was one level away from becoming a United States citizen. This immigrant status was very difficult to obtain, and we had acquired it while still in Liberia. I was extremely grateful that God had made a way out of Liberia for my family and me. We would finally be able to leave the devastation in Liberia and move to the United States where there was safety and stability. On that day I felt like I was floating in the clouds.

Nightmare Returns

Pretty soon, news of my family winning the diversity visa lottery spread throughout my neighborhood and school. We soon became the center of attention and the envy of the community. Most people in my community were looking for a way out because they all knew that Liberia was very unstable. The reality was that even if the war miraculously ended, it would take many years for Liberia to be what it used to be. I did not believe that Liberia could ever truly return to its prewar state. I would hope that it might probably get better, but the reality is that it would likely get worse. How could Liberia be the same again when so many lives had been lost and we had all been exposed to so many atrocities? How could I see Liberia like I used to when I had no closure as to the whereabouts of my mother? So this answered prayer was going to be good for me. I believed that it was going to be good for my entire family. We all needed a fresh start, and this would definitely be obtained by our relocation to the United States.

I was in a very good mood in spite of all that was going on around me. I was focusing more on my relationship with God, especially after I had experienced God answering a major prayer. My faith increased so much as a result of that answered prayer. The God who was faithful enough to answer my prayer by making my family win the diversity visa lottery could also be faithful enough to make a way for my family to travel to the United States. I had to have faith because we had many hurdles ahead of us. Winning the diversity visa lottery was step one. However, we had to meet other requirements to be able to enjoy the benefits of winning the diversity visa lottery.

First, we needed the funds to pay for the various processing fees. Most importantly, we had to have a sponsor to host us after we arrive in the United States. This was one of the biggest hurdles that we needed to overcome. No sponsor (affidavit of support), no trip to the United States. We also needed to successfully make it through the interviews and vetting process, which I was not that concerned about. The final hurdle was getting the funds to purchase the tickets for all of us. For a family of four, this would cost several thousand United States dollars. My father did okay, but he did not have thousands of United States dollars laying around. I should have been worried about all of this, but I wasn't. I trusted that the God who answered my prayers would make a way for my family to get the funds to purchase our airfare.

Shortly after my family won the diversity visa lottery, tension started to build up in Monrovia between the various warring factions. It was obviously concerning to me, but I was not very concern about the tension. This was just a way of life in war-torn Liberia. Most of the time, the tension did not lead to fighting. Even if a fight broke out, it usually lasted for a brief period. I was too excited about my plans to leave Liberia. Therefore, I did not allow the many negative situations in Liberia to occupy my mind.

One quiet morning, at approximately 5:00 a.m., I was studying for a biology test that I was expecting. The date of this incident was April 6, 1996. While I was cramming information into my brain in preparation for the test, I heard loud knocking on the back door. It was a strange time of the morning for anyone to be knocking on the door of my home. I rightfully guessed that whoever was knocking on the back door was someone who was familiar to our family. Strangers usually knocked on our front door. So I went to the back door and saw one of our neighbors at the door. He asked me if I heard the gunfire and if we were okay. Actually, I did not hear the shooting. I was too involved in my studies to hear the sound of guns firing. As I focused on the sound of the gun firing, I started to hear it slightly.

Now I was worried, my fears were no longer imaginary. Instead, my fears were quickly becoming a reality. When it seemed like hope was so close, it appeared to be getting snatched right out of my hands. My father who had also awakened quickly ran to the hospital to find out what was happening. His bosses had access to information, and they were often able to provide reliable information. While my father was gathering information at the hospital, my brothers and I quickly gathered some clothes and food to take with us in case we had to relocate. This was one of the lessons that we had come to learn because of our previous experience of living in a civil war environment. Because of the uncertainties of war, one always wanted to have their personal items ready to travel if an exigent circumstance developed. My father later returned home from the hospital and told us to quickly follow him to the St. Joseph Catholic Hospital. We followed my father to the hospital compound, which was gated and probably one of the safest places in Monrovia. It was considered safe, not only because it was gated but it was also protected by ECOMOG peacekeepers. We all went to my father's best friend's house to seek refuge. My father's best friend resided in the confines of the St. Joseph Catholic Hospital because he was the medical director at the hospital. We sought refuge on the hospital premises with another family that was also very close to us. This was our best choice since we did not have the opportunity to fly out of Liberia at the time. The only other way out of Monrovia was by sea. Many people attempted to flee Monrovia for neighboring nations on the few ships that were available. So many individuals were desperate and placed their lives at risk for an opportunity to flee Monrovia. In fact some of those individuals even lost their lives by drowning while attempting to board ships and flee Monrovia. I guess that the words spoken by Charles Taylor and his supporters during Operation Octopus finally manifested into reality. They were finally able to flush some of those living in Monrovia into the sea. This was very unfortunate since we were all Liberians tearing each other apart. However, I was glad that I was able to find refuge behind the protection of the ECOMOG peacekeepers. Thanks to my father's best friend assisting my family. The practice of helping others in need was also very common in Liberia. I believe that because most Liberians could relate to being in need, it was easier for most Liberians to provide assistance if they could do so.

Now I believed that we were saved. After all, we had the protection of the ECOMOG peacekeepers, and nothing could happen to us. However, the rapid sound of machine gun firing started to get closer to us. At first, it did not seem like we benefitted much by seeking refuge within the gates of the St. Joseph Catholic Hospital compound. The sound of rapid gun firing was now upon us. I could hear the sounds of soldier's boots walking around the house that I was seeking shelter in. I immediately had flashback of my initial experience in the beginning of the civil war that occurred in 1990. The fears that I developed due to the atrocities that I experienced were all coming back to me. As I lay on the floor, seeking cover from the bullets that were flying around me, I started to think of the real possibility that I could lose an opportunity of a lifetime. If my family relocated as a result of the fighting that was going on, we would likely be unable to complete the process required to migrate to the United States. Just a few weeks earlier I was so pumped with excitement that I finally had a way out of Liberia. Now it appeared that I had been sucked right back into the unlimited devastation of the Liberian civil war. In the mist of desperation with nowhere to turn, I started to say a silent prayer. I asked God to protect us all as we sought refuge. I also prayed that the fighting would stop. These gunfights normally lead to loss of many lives. Personally, this fight would also cost me to miss on an opportunity to migrate to the United States, and I did not want to miss such an opportunity. The gunfight continued for several hours. At times, the fighting intensified. I was really afraid because I did not know what was going on. Normally, I would have some idea of the reason for the fight. For example, one warring faction fighting against another warring faction. However, in this case, all of warring factions were part of the interim government. Therefore, they were not fighting to capture territories as they often did. Eventually, I learned that the fighting was more about making a political maneuver. Sadly, a political maneuver would result in the destruction of properties and lives. After several hours of intensive gunfight, there was absolute quietness. It appeared that the soldiers had gone away suddenly. I was relieved that the fighting had ended. At least, this was the case in my immediate neighborhood. I am sure that other neighborhoods were still dealing with the sound of gunfire. I could still hear the sound of gunfire in other communities. I was glad that during this battle I did not encounter General "Butt Naked." He was a major participant in this fight. He was feared by many, including myself. He gained his nickname because he was known to not wear clothes. He went to battle while naked, and his only weapon was a machete. He was known to be brutal. He brutally murdered his opponents and innocent civilians by hacking them to death. He was known to utilize powerful juju (black magic) for his protection and power. I heard many horrific tales of General "Butt Naked," and I did not wish to encounter him. I had already met two of the most dangerous generals in the Liberian civil war, and I really did not want to meet this one. Thank God that I did not encounter him in this recent fighting.

God was faithful once more, and he answered my prayer, and I'm quite sure the prayers of many. The fighting stopped, and an agreement was made between the various warring factions. After the fighting ended, life seemed to have picked up right where it left off. I returned to school; however, I learned that my school would end the school year early. It seemed like many of the schools decided to end their school year early. I guessed that the coming presidential election was a concern. It had always been the case in Liberia that presidential election brought about instability. I also received one of the most devastating news that still saddens me today. After receiving my report card, I also learned that St. Patrick's High School would be shutting down permanently. This news devastated me because I had become very connected to the institution. I had spent almost all of my teenage life at St. Patrick's high school, and it was sad that the school would no longer exist. While I knew that I would not have graduated from St. Patrick's due to my expected migration to the United States, I wanted others to have the opportunity to enjoy and experience the same things that I experienced. The war had once more taken something away from me that was important. I believe that had I not already had plans to travel to the United States this would have been even more devastating for me. I believed that the staff at St. Patrick's High School had also been beaten down to the point of no return, a result of the impact of the civil war in Liberia.

The Exit

After the most recent outbreak of fighting, life quickly returned to normal once again. I guess we had become accustomed to the on-again-off-again atmosphere that we were living in. When you do not have much of a choice, you adapt to your situation. I also had to get back up and keep moving forward with life. I saw this exercised around me; therefore, I gained strength from those around me. With a little time left for me to exit Liberia, I decided to live cautiously. Now that the warring faction members were in Monrovia, I decided to stay close to school. The fact is that anything could happen in Monrovia. The fighting that broke out on April 6 was a revelation that Monrovia was not stable due to the warring factions' representatives and their supporters residing in the city. Therefore, when it was time to return to school, we had to look for a new school. I spoke with my brothers and presented the idea of attending a school that was close to our home. I realized that none of the schools in my community were schools that my brothers and I would prefer. Most of the good schools that we preferred were located in inner city of Monrovia. However, I advised my brothers to stay close to home in the case that we had to return home quickly as a result of some uncertainty. My brothers agreed to my suggestion, and we informed our father about our decision. We asked our father to allow us to enroll in the Assembly of God (AGM) School. This school was very close to our home, and we could likely get home if there was any emergency. So my father agreed with our concerns and enrolled us in the Assembly of God High School. We traded preference for safety. My experience at the school was actually better than I expected. During my time at my new school, I was able to make the varsity basketball team. I even earned a full athletic scholarship. My team also became a dominant high school basketball team that season. I also did very well academically. I was one of the top three students in my class. I also made lot of great friends, and I enjoyed my overall experience at the school.

As we prepared to relocate to the United States, I continued to experience God working in the life of my family. My father had some hurdles to overcome and make our dream of travelling to the United States a reality. My father still needed to gather enough funds to purchase our plane tickets. He also had to find someone who could accommodate our family (affidavit of support). These were no easy challenges. Although we did not have the resources needed to overcome those requirements, my father acted on faith. He did what he was able to do. He sold some of the valuables in our home such as our furniture, music equipment, and my mother's jewelries. He also sold the land that he and my mother purchased. I saw my father work really hard to secure the funds needed to purchase our airfare. After my father did all that he could to secure the airfare, he turned to his employers at the hospital to borrow what he was lacking. Through God's divine intervention, his employers were more than willing to give him the funds as a gift in appreciation for his hard work over the years and for the risk that he took after we had returned home from the initial fighting in 1990 to protect the hospital property. However, his employers really did not want him to leave. He gained the trust of his employers, and he ran the hospital successfully. His employers initially asked if my father could send us to family members in the United States. However, my father could not because we had lost connection with our relatives in the United States. They also offered to find a Catholic organization that would host my brothers and me in the United States. My father insisted that he was not comfortable with sending us to a strange land alone, especially after being involuntarily separated from our mother. Finally, my father's employers asked if he could find and train a replacement for his position at the hospital. My father was able to do that. He found a trusted former colleague and took him to his employers.

My father was also able to find a sponsor in the United States through his other employer at the SMA Guest House. One of the priests at the SMA Guest House was an American, and he was able to connect my father with another priest in the United States who used to reside in Liberia. Now we could breathe a sigh of relief. We had overcome all the hurdles that were ahead of us. We were now simply waiting for school to close. It all seemed surreal to me that I was leaving Liberia for the United States through winning a visa lottery. It all became real to me when my father and I went to purchase the plane ticket at the travel agency. After purchasing the plane tickets, we were driving back home when the song "I Believe I Can Fly" by R. Kelly began to play on the radio. My father and I looked at one another and started to laugh. We both agreed that this was confirmation that we would indeed travel safely to the United States. This confirmation brought about a good feeling. It was needed in an unstable place like Liberia. The instability of Liberia was always a concern with regards to traveling out of Liberia. At any time, a gunfight could occur, and our plans to travel to the United States could be hindered. This was a very real possibility since the presidential election was right around the corner. There were concerns among some Liberians that things could become ugly if Charles Taylor did not win the presidential election. Surprisingly to me, Charles Taylor was able to gain the support of many Liberians. His road to the seat of power was very possible at this point. I witness the support of Charles Taylor during his wedding to Jewel Howard. I could not believe the level of excitement and support that so many Liberians had for Charles Taylor. It almost seemed like the crimes against humanity that Charles Taylor brought upon Liberia had been wiped away. This bizarre support for Charles Taylor was also fully displayed during one of his political campaign rallies. I saw hundreds of Liberians running through the streets of Monrovia chanting, "You kill my ma, you kill my pa, I will vote for you." I could not believe my eyes and ears as I witnessed hundreds of Liberians run along Tubman Boulevard chanting this disturbing slogan. I reasoned that some of those who I witnessed chanting in the streets were doing so out of fear that Charles Taylor would create more problems if he did not win the presidential elections. Everyone could see that Charles Taylor was going to win the presidential elections in Liberia. I saw that as more future problems for Liberia.

As it got closer to the elections, things became a little tense. During that time, I decided not to vote in the elections. I made this decision because I was going to be leaving Liberia and I did not believe that it was right for me to make a decision to vote for a leader in a nation that I would not be living in. Although I would soon be leaving Liberia, I was hopeful for the nation and its people. I also hoped and prayed that the election would go on successfully in spite of the leader that Liberians would elect.

On the morning of the election, things seemed to be going on smoothly. There was a sense of optimism in the air. There also appeared to be some improvement in Liberia. For the first time since the war began, the local television station started to broadcast. I was able to watch some parts of the election process on television. By the mercy of God, the election process successfully concluded without any fighting. At the end of the election process, Charles Taylor won the election as most expected.

This was a very disappointing election result for me. However, I was glad that the election went on without any chaos or gunfights between the different warring factions. As for me, I felt that Charles Taylor was going to continue his brutal leadership style. However, the people had spoken, and there was not a thing I could do about it. So I continued to prepare for my exit trip out of Liberia.

During my last days in Liberia, many relatives and friends came to visit my family home. My maternal aunt also surprisingly showed up one evening at my home. She informed us that she had heard of our good news and that she came to see us before we could leave Liberia. Her presence brought back much memories of my mother since they held such resemblance. In fact, because of their resemblance, my younger brother thought that it was our mother who was approaching us when he initially saw our aunt. It certainly felt good to see so many of my close relatives and friends as we prepared to leave Liberia. Of all those who visited our home, one of them had the most important impact in my life. During one of many times that my family had visitors, one of my father's friend stopped by to visit my father. While he was visiting, he learned that I was struggling with an illness. So my father's friend inquired about my illness. After speaking with my father about my illness, he told my father that he had some herbs that could help me. My father's friend stated that he was once an apprentice for a natural herbalist and that he had a herb that could heal me. He told my father that he would go and look for the herb. He promised to return with the herb. After several hours of waiting, my father's friend returned with some leaves preserved in dry mud. According to my father's friend, the herb was very reliable and could cure most illness. Unfortunately, he informed us that he did not know where to find the herb leaves. He informed us that his teacher passed away before teaching him where to find the herb. As God would have it, my father's friend preserved the last herb that he had in dry mud. I was given the dry mud and instructed to eat it. The herb was mixed into the dry mud. I was instructed to stay close to home after chewing the herb because I would be making frequent trips to the toilet. Therefore, I followed the instructions of my father's friend. I stayed home for several hours. After waiting for several hours, I concluded that the herb was not going to work. So I left for town to continue doing my shopping. I went to town and completed my shopping. As I attempted to catch a cab and return home, I felt my stomach rumbling. I had no public restroom to ease myself. Therefore, I had to catch a cab and return home before I had an accident. After making multiple attempts to catch a cab, I was successful. However, the ride home was an awful experience. As I was attempting to stop myself from having an accident on the bus, the bus bounced in just about every pothole that it came across. During the ride, I almost give up. I thought I was going to embarrass myself. Fortunately for me, I made it home safely without any mishap. After returning home, I started to vomit forcefully. I threw up so much that I felt exhausted when it was all over. I threw up what looked like raw egg yolks. It was a lot of them. At the end of this experience, I stayed home and rested myself. As time went by, I noticed that my illness did not resurface. I had no fever or weakness. I did not lose consciousness or experienced seizure. It seemed like I finally had a cure for my illness. I was grateful to God for providing me the opportunity to cross paths with my father's friend. I had been dealing with this challenge for the previous five years, and it seemed like the cycle of this illness in my life was finally over.

At the end of my stay in Liberia, my father was rewarded by his employers at St. Joseph Catholic Hospital. Brother Jose, Brother Justino, and the staff at St. Joseph Catholic Hospital held a ceremony to honor my father in appreciation for his service to the hospital and the community. I learned a very valuable lesson from my father about being patient and waiting on God's time. I had always felt like my father was been shortened by others or that he had shortened himself. He shortened himself when he declined free housing with electricity and water. He was shortened when he did not get the pay he was supposed to receive at his position as personal director of the hospital. Now God was rewarding him in a big way. God rewarded him at the right time when the reward would have the most impact in his life. I will cherish this lesson forever.

On the day that I was finally leaving Liberia for the United States, a few of my close family and friends escorted us to the airport. It was such a joyous moment for my family. I was excited to be finally moving to the United States. In spite of the feeling of excitement, it was also a bittersweet moment. It was sad to leave my friends and relatives who I had known all of my life. Most frustrating was that my family was leaving Liberia without mother and our unknown sibling. I did not know if my mother was dead or alive. I often wondered if I had another sibling out there, probably a sister. There was no way to know the answer to any of these questions. However, I was leaving to start a new chapter in my life, a new chapter of hope.

When it was time for me to leave Liberia, I became a little anxious. I was still fearful that anything could happen to keep us from leaving Liberia. At the time, I could not think of any reason why our flight would be prevented from leaving. However, years of uncertainties had built up enough fear in me to make me become irrational. My family eventually boarded our plane along with my aunt and my neighbor's daughter who we were chaperoning.

As the plane took off, I looked back and saw the land that I've known all of my life fade away. It all seemed surreal. I wondered how it came to be that I was now so eager to leave behind the land that I grew up loving. The land that I had so many fond memories of became a land that I now had nightmares about. Liberia was supposed to be an oasis for free slaves. The free land of liberty. An oasis where free slaves would bring their skills and work together with their indigenous brothers and sisters to build a successful community. Instead, many free slaves who migrated to Liberia decided to portray similar ill treatments that their slave masters inflicted upon them. I guess our sinful natural instincts led us to a path of wickedness. "For I know that nothing good dwells in me that is in my flesh (Rom 7:18a ESV). The offenses that occurred in the Liberian history brought a lot of pain between both sides. Pain led to anger, and anger led to hate. Hate eventually led to malice, which led to the destruction that I experienced during the Liberia civil war. Unforgiveness can be powerful if allowed to grow. "Be angry and sin not: let not the sun go down on your wrath" (Eph. 4:26 ESV). Unfortunately, as Liberians, we give breath to our anger, which lead us to express our anger through brutal violence. Neither gives place to the devil (Eph. 4:27 ESV). Two wrong actions certainly cannot produce good results. I am hoping that as Liberians, we can turn away from our pain and anger and exercise forgiveness. It is only through the power of God that we can accomplish this. I can do all things through him who strengthens me (Phil. 4:13 ESV). I believe that Liberia can overcome its history of pain and anger and become the nation that it was meant to be. I left Liberia sad but optimistic that one day I would return.

(1997 - Dad Farewell Celebration)

(1997 - Dad Farewell Celebration)

(1997 - Dad Farewell Celebration)

Bibliography

Bayard, Samuel. *A Sketch of the Life of Commodore Robert F. Stockton.* New York: Derby & Jackson, 1856.

Dunn-Marcos, Robin, et al. *Liberians: An Introduction to their History and Culture*, 2005.

Harris, Karen. "Liberia's 1927 Presidential Election: The Most Rigged Election Ever (with a 1,680% Turnout)." Last modified September 21, 2020. https://historydaily.org/liberia-1927-presidential-election-most-rigged-election-ever/2.

Huffman, Alan. *Mississippi in Africa: The Saga of the Slaves of Prospect Hill Plantation and Their Legacy in Liberia Today, First Edition.* Wyoming: Gotham Books, 2004.

The ESV Bible. Crossway, 2023, www.esv.org.

About the Author

Quemiline is a husband of a beautiful wife and four wonderful daughters. He has served others for most of his adult life. From the military to law enforcement and in many capacities in churches and his community, he continues to serve. Quemiline has served in various leader roles in various churches for over fifteen years. Some of the roles he had served include head of security and men's group leader. He also enjoys teaching the Bible. When Quemiline is not serving his family, church, or community, he enjoys working out and playing sports. He also enjoys traveling, and he enjoys hot sunny beaches where the beauty of God's creation is in full display.

Quemiline was born and raised in Monrovia, Liberia. After migrating to the United States, Quemiline lived in several states before settling in South Central, Pennsylvania, where he enjoys the beautiful country living.

Printed in the USA
CPSIA information can be obtained
at www.ICGtesting.com
CBHW040704181124
17562CB00039B/397